AF712283

HEALTH CARE ISSUES, COSTS AND ACCESS

MANDATED HEALTH CARE: CONSTITUTIONAL ANALYSIS

Health Care Issues, Costs and Access

Additional books in this series can be found on Nova's website under the Series tab.

Additional E-books in this series can be found on Nova's website under the E-books tab.

Congressional Policies, Practices and Procedures

Additional books in this series can be found on Nova's website under the Series tab.

Additional E-books in this series can be found on Nova's website under the E-books tab.

HEALTH CARE ISSUES, COSTS AND ACCESS

MANDATED HEALTH CARE: CONSTITUTIONAL ANALYSIS

JONATHAN P. REILLY
EDITOR

Nova Science Publishers, Inc.
New York

Copyright © 2011 by Nova Science Publishers, Inc.

All rights reserved. No part of this book may be reproduced, stored in a retrieval system or transmitted in any form or by any means: electronic, electrostatic, magnetic, tape, mechanical photocopying, recording or otherwise without the written permission of the Publisher.

For permission to use material from this book please contact us:
Telephone 631-231-7269; Fax 631-231-8175
Web Site: http://www.novapublishers.com

NOTICE TO THE READER

The Publisher has taken reasonable care in the preparation of this book, but makes no expressed or implied warranty of any kind and assumes no responsibility for any errors or omissions. No liability is assumed for incidental or consequential damages in connection with or arising out of information contained in this book. The Publisher shall not be liable for any special, consequential, or exemplary damages resulting, in whole or in part, from the readers' use of, or reliance upon, this material. Any parts of this book based on government reports are so indicated and copyright is claimed for those parts to the extent applicable to compilations of such works.

Independent verification should be sought for any data, advice or recommendations contained in this book. In addition, no responsibility is assumed by the publisher for any injury and/or damage to persons or property arising from any methods, products, instructions, ideas or otherwise contained in this publication.

This publication is designed to provide accurate and authoritative information with regard to the subject matter covered herein. It is sold with the clear understanding that the Publisher is not engaged in rendering legal or any other professional services. If legal or any other expert assistance is required, the services of a competent person should be sought. FROM A DECLARATION OF PARTICIPANTS JOINTLY ADOPTED BY A COMMITTEE OF THE AMERICAN BAR ASSOCIATION AND A COMMITTEE OF PUBLISHERS.

Additional color graphics may be available in the e-book version of this book.

Library of Congress Cataloging-in-Publication Data

Mandated health care : constitutional analysis / editor, Jonathan P. Reilly.
p. cm.
Includes reprints of reports prepared by the Congressional Research Service.
Includes bibliographical references and index.
ISBN 978-1-61324-162-2 (softcover)
1. Compulsory health insurance--Law and legislation--United States. 2. United States. Patient Protection and Affordable Care Act. I. Reilly, Jonathan P. II. Library of Congress. Congressional Research Service.
[DNLM: 1. United States. Patient Protection and Affordable Care Act. 2. Government Regulation--United States. 3. Insurance, Health--legislation & jurisprudence--United States. 4. Health Care Reform--legislation & jurisprudence--United States. 5. Human Rights--United States. 6. Mandatory Programs--legislation & jurisprudence--United States. W 32.5 AA1]
KF3605.M26 2011
344.7302'2--dc22

2011009067

Published by Nova Science Publishers, Inc. ✝ New York

CONTENTS

PREFACE

The health care reform debate raises many complex issues including those of coverage, accessibility, cost, accountability and quality of health care. Underlying these policy considerations are issues regarding the status of health care as a constitutional or legal right. This new book analyzes constitutional and legal issues pertaining to a right to health care, as well as the power of Congress to enact and fund health care programs. Following the recent passage of the Patient Protection and Affordable Care Act, legal issues have been raised regarding the power of Congress to mandate that individuals purchase health insurance, and the ability of states to "nullify" or "opt out" of such a requirement.

Chapter 1- The health care reform debate raises many complex issues including those of coverage, accessibility, cost, accountability, and quality of health care. Underlying these policy considerations are issues regarding the status of health care as a constitutional or legal right. This report analyzes constitutional and legal issues pertaining to a right to health care, as well as the power of Congress to enact and fund health care programs. Following the recent passage of the Patient Protection and Affordable Care Act, P.L. 111-148, legal issues have been raised regarding the power of Congress to mandate that individuals purchase health insurance, and the ability of states to “nullify” or “opt out” of such a requirement. These issues are also discussed.

Chapter 2- As part of the Patient Protection and Affordable Care Act, P.L. 111-148, as amended, Congress enacted an “minimum essential coverage requirement,” a provision compelling certain individuals to have a minimum level of health insurance (i.e., an “individual mandate”). Individuals who fail to do so are subject to a monetary penalty, administered through the tax code.

Although the federal government provides health coverage for many individuals through federal programs such as Medicare, it had never before required individuals to purchase health insurance.

Chapter 3- Pursuant to Rule 15(a), Federal Rules of Civil Procedure, Plaintiffs file this Second Amended Complaint against Defendants and state:

Chapter 4- In March 2010, Congress enacted the Patient Protection and Affordable Care Act (PPACA), which included a provision that requires certain individuals to have a minimum level of health insurance. Additionally, the threat of bioterrorism has caused some to consider the possibility of introducing vaccination programs to prevent an outbreak of serious illnesses. Programs like health care coverage and vaccinations have the potential to violate certain religious beliefs and therefore may conflict with the First Amendment. In the continuing debate over issues for which mandatory health care programs might be solutions, questions have been raised about the constitutional issues relating to exemptions for health care programs.

In: Mandated Health Care: Constitutional Analysis ISBN: 978-1-61324-162-2
Editor: Jonathan P. Reilly © 2011 Nova Science Publishers, Inc.

Chapter 1

HEALTH CARE: CONSTITUTIONAL RIGHTS AND LEGISLATIVE POWERS*

Kathleen S. Swendiman

SUMMARY

The health care reform debate raises many complex issues including those of coverage, accessibility, cost, accountability, and quality of health care. Underlying these policy considerations are issues regarding the status of health care as a constitutional or legal right. This report analyzes constitutional and legal issues pertaining to a right to health care, as well as the power of Congress to enact and fund health care programs. Following the recent passage of the Patient Protection and Affordable Care Act, P.L. 111-148, legal issues have been raised regarding the power of Congress to mandate that individuals purchase health insurance, and the ability of states to "nullify" or "opt out" of such a requirement. These issues are also discussed.

The U.S. Constitution does not set forth an explicit right to health care. While the Supreme Court would likely find that the Constitution provides a right to obtain health care services at one's own expense from willing providers, the Supreme Court has never interpreted the Constitution as

* This is an edited, reformatted and augmented version of a Congressional Research Services publication, dated December 30, 2010.

guaranteeing a right to health care services from the government for those who cannot afford it. The Supreme Court has, however, held that the government has an obligation to provide medical care in certain limited circumstances, such as for prisoners.

While the U.S. Constitution and Supreme Court interpretations do not identify a constitutional right to health care for those who cannot afford it, Congress has enacted numerous statutes, such as Medicare, Medicaid, and the Children's Health Insurance Program, that establish and define specific statutory rights of individuals to receive health care services from the government. As a major component of many health care entitlement statutes, Congress has provided funding to pay for the health services provided under law. Most of these statutes have been enacted pursuant to Congress's authority to "make all Laws which shall be necessary and proper" to carry out its mandate "to ... provide for the ... general Welfare." The power to spend for the general welfare is one of the broadest grants of authority to Congress in the U.S. Constitution. The Supreme Court accords considerable deference to a legislative decision by Congress that a particular health care spending program provides for the general welfare.

Recently, Congress enacted comprehensive health care reform legislation, P.L. 111-148, which includes a requirement, effective in 2014, that individuals purchase health insurance, and which significantly expands the Medicaid program. A number of lawsuits have been filed challenging various provisions of this legislation, including the power of Congress to enact an individual mandate to purchase health insurance under the Commerce Clause or other provisions of the U.S. Constitution. These lawsuits are in various stages of litigation, and it is expected that one or more of these cases will eventually reach the Supreme Court. In addition, several states have passed laws, or amended their state constitutions, to attempt to "nullify" or "opt out" of the federal individual health insurance mandate. Direct conflicts between federal and state laws, and state constitutional amendments, would raise constitutional issues which are likely to be resolved in favor of federal law under the Supremacy Clause of the U.S. Constitution.

A number of state constitutions contain provisions relating to health and the provision of health care services. State constitutions may provide constitutional rights that are more expansive than those found under the federal Constitution since federal rights set the minimum standards for the states.

HEALTH CARE RIGHTS UNDER THE U.S. CONSTITUTION

The health care reform debate raises many complex issues including those of coverage, accessibility, cost, accountability, and quality of health care. Underlying these policy considerations are issues regarding the status of health or health care as a moral, legal, or constitutional right. It may be useful to distinguish between a right to health and a right to health care.[1] An often cited definition of "health" from the World Health Organization describes health as "a state of complete physical, mental and social wellbeing and not merely the absence of disease or infirmity."[2] "Health care" connotes the means for the achievement of health, as in the "care, services or supplies related to the health of an individual."[3] For purposes of this report, discussion will be limited to constitutional and legal issues pertaining to a right to health care.

Numerous questions arise concerning the parameters of a "right to health care." If each individual has a right to health care, how much care does a person have a right to and from whom? Would equality of access be a component of such a right? Do federal or state governments have a duty to provide health care services to the large numbers of medically uninsured persons? What kind of health care system would fulfill a duty to provide health care? How should this duty be enforced? The debate on these and other questions may be informed by a summary of the scope of the right to health care, particularly the right to access health care paid for by the government, under the U.S. Constitution and interpretations of the U.S. Supreme Court.[4]

Explicit Rights in the U.S. Constitution

The United States Constitution does not explicitly address a right to health care. The words "health" or "medical care" do not appear anywhere in the text of the Constitution. The provisions in the Constitution indicate that the framers were somewhat more concerned with guaranteeing freedom *from* government, rather than with providing for specific rights to governmental services such as for health care. The right to a jury trial, the writ of habeas corpus, protection for contracts, and protection against ex post facto laws were among the few individual rights explicitly set forth in the original Constitution.[5] In 1791, the Bill of Rights was added to the Constitution, and additional amendments were added following the Civil War, and thereafter. Most constitutional amendments dealt with civil and political rights, not social and economic rights.[6] However, there have been proposals to add a specific right to health care as an amendment to the U.S. Constitution. For example, in 1944, President Franklin D. Roosevelt, in his State of the Union address, advanced his idea of a "Second Bill of Rights" which would include "[t]he right to adequate medical care and the opportunity to achieve and enjoy good health."[7] More recently, Representative Jesse L. Jackson Jr. introduced H.J.Res. 30 on March 3, 2009, a bill which proposes an amendment to the U.S. Constitution ensuring a right to health care. The proposed amendment reads, "Section 1. All persons shall enjoy the right to health care of equal high quality. Section 2. The Congress shall have power to enforce and implement this article by appropriate legislation."

The Right to Health Care at the Government's Expense

Even though the U.S. Constitution does not explicitly set forth a right to health care, the Supreme Court's decisions in the areas of the right to privacy and bodily integrity suggest the Constitution implicitly provides an individual the right to access health care services at one's own expense from willing medical providers.[8] However, issues regarding access to health care do not usually concern access where a person has the means and ability to pay for health care, but rather involve situations where a person cannot afford to pay for health care. The question becomes, not whether one has a right to health care that one can pay for, but whether the government or some other entity has the obligation to provide such care to those who cannot afford it.

If the Supreme Court were to find an implicit right to health care for persons unable to pay for such care, it might do so either by finding that the Constitution implicitly guarantees such a right, or that a law which treats persons differently based on financial need creates a "suspect classification." In either case, the Court would evaluate the constitutionality of legislative enactments that unduly burden such rights or classifications under its "strict scrutiny" standard of review, thus according the highest level of constitutional protection offered by the equal protection guarantees of the Constitution. Absent a finding of an implicit fundamental right to health care for poor persons under the Constitution, or that wealth distinctions create a "suspect class," the Court would likely evaluate governmental actions involving health care using the less rigorous "rational basis" standard of review. Most health care legislation would likely be upheld, as it has been, so long as the government can show that the legislation bears a rational relationship to a legitimate governmental interest.

Substantive Due Process: Impact on Fundamental Rights

Despite the lack of discussion of health care rights in the Constitution, arguments have been made that the denial by the federal government of a minimal level of health care to poor persons transgresses the equal protection guarantees under the Constitution. While the equal protection clause of the Fourteenth Amendment applies only to the states, similar equal protection principles are applicable to the federal government through the Due Process Clause of the Fifth Amendment.[9] A litigant challenging a federal action has the burden of proving that the governmental action places an undue burden on the exercise of an individual's fundamental right. The standard of review used in cases involving fundamental rights is called "strict scrutiny." Using this heightened standard of review, if the Court determines that a fundamental right has been unduly burdened, the governmental action will only be upheld if the government can demonstrate that the action is necessary to achieve a compelling governmental interest.[10]

The Supreme Court has held that the Due Process Clause of the Fourteenth Amendment provides constitutional protection for certain rights or "liberty interests" related to privacy.[11] Legislative enactments that implicate the right to privacy have been reviewed under the heightened strict scrutiny standard of review. Thus, the right to privacy has been held to include the right to procreate,[12] use contraception,[13] have an abortion,[14] and maintain bodily integrity.[15]

While the Supreme Court has held that the Constitution implicitly confers a fundamental right to privacy, the Court has not elevated health care to the status of a fundamental right. The Court has evaluated governmental actions involving health care using the less rigorous "rational basis" standard of review. Under this standard, a governmental action will be upheld if the action bears a rational relationship to a legitimate governmental interest.[16] For example, in *Maher v. Roe*,[17] the Supreme Court held that a state could refuse to provide public assistance for non-therapeutic abortions under a program that subsidized all medical expenses otherwise associated with pregnancy and childbirth. In other words, while the constitutional right to an abortion protected a woman's right to choose whether or not to terminate a pregnancy, it did not mean abortion was a health right.[18]

In *Harris v. McRae*,[19] the Supreme Court held that the Medicaid program's refusal, under the Hyde Amendment, to pay for medically necessary abortions did not burden a woman's fundamental right to choose an abortion. The Court applied the rational basis standard of review and found that poor pregnant women were not denied equal protection of the laws because the abortion provisions were rationally related to a governmental "interest in protecting the potential life of the fetus."[20] The Court also noted that while the Due Process Clause of the Fourteenth Amendment affords protection against unwarranted government interference with freedom of choice regarding certain personal decisions, it "does not confer an entitlement to such funds as may be necessary to realize all the advantages of that freedom."[21] The Court stated further,[22]

> To translate the limitation on government power implicit in the Due Process Clause into an affirmative funding obligation would require Congress to subsidize the medically necessary abortion of an indigent woman even if Congress had not enacted a Medicaid program to subsidize other medically necessary services. Nothing in the Due Process Clause supports such an extraordinary result. Whether freedom of choice that is constitutionally protected warrants federal subsidization is a question for Congress to answer, not a matter of constitutional entitlement.

In other words, a woman has a constitutional right to terminate her pregnancy, but that right is not unduly burdened if she cannot afford an abortion.[23] More broadly, the Constitution does not obligate the states or the federal government to pay for medical expenses, even for the health care of poor persons.[24]

The Court's use of the rational basis test for constitutional analyses of health care legislation extends to other, related areas, such as housing[25] and education.[26] In the welfare area, the Court has, at times, acknowledged the importance of public assistance to poor persons. In *Goldberg v. Kelly*,[27] where the Court held that due process rights attach to welfare benefits, the Court stated,[28]

> From its founding the Nation's basic commitment has been to foster the dignity and wellbeing of all persons within its borders.... Welfare, by meeting the basic demands of subsistence, can help bring within the reach of the poor the same opportunities that are available to others to participate meaningfully in the life of the community.... Public assistance, then is not mere charity, but a means to "promote the general Welfare, and secure the Blessings of Liberty to ourselves and our Posterity."

While the Court recognized the state's duty to meet the basic needs of its citizens, it declined to impose an affirmative duty to do so, making it clear that welfare is not a constitutional right, and the state does not have an obligation to provide resources to meet subsistence needs.[29]

Equal Protection: Wealth as a "Suspect Class"

For a classification that treats people differently—such as health care services for some poor persons but not all who are in need—to rise to the highest level of constitutional protection, the classification must be found to be a "suspect classification" by the Supreme Court. According to the Court, the constitutional guarantee of equal protection is not a source of substantive rights, but rather a "right to be free from invidious discrimination in statutory classifications and other governmental activity."[30] In cases where the Court determines state or federal governmental classifications to be "suspect," it will apply the strict scrutiny standard of review. Thus, the Court has applied the strict scrutiny test to suspect classifications based on race,[31] ethnicity,[32] and national origin.[33]

The High Court, however, has not seen fit to consider financial need or distinctions on the basis of wealth as suspect classifications for purposes of its equal protection analysis.[34] For example, in *Dandridge v. Williams*,[35] the Court upheld a Maryland welfare distribution scheme whereby an upper limit was placed on the amount of assistance any one family could receive. This meant that larger families with greater need received less aid per child than smaller families. The Court stated the following:[36]

> In the area of economics and social welfare a State does not violate the Equal Protection Clause merely because the classifications made by its laws are imperfect. If the classification has some "rational basis," it does not offend the Constitution simply because the classification "is not made with mathematical nicety or because in practice it results in some inequality."

Thus, the Court concluded that while the Constitution may require procedural safeguards for the distribution of economic and social welfare benefits, as it held in *Goldberg v. Kelly*, it "does not empower this Court to second-guess state officials charged with the difficult responsibility of allocating limited public welfare funds among the myriad of potential recipients."[37] The Court has reaffirmed this holding in subsequent cases.[38] In like manner, in the health care area, the Court has again applied the more deferential "rational basis" standard of review in assessing the constitutionality of distinctions or classifications in the provision of health care on the basis of wealth. Health care legislation will generally be upheld so long as the government can show a legitimate purpose and a rational basis for carrying out the program.

Exception: Under Government Control

The Supreme Court has held that, under certain circumstances, persons under governmental control, such that they are dependent upon the government for their basic needs, have a right to a minimal amount of medical care. However, the Supreme Court has not based its decisions defining a right to medical care for persons with limited freedoms on a fundamental right to health care.[39] Rather, in the case of prisoners, the Supreme Court has held that they are entitled to adequate food, clothing, shelter, and medical care as a component of the protections accorded by the Eighth Amendment.[40] "[D]eliberate indifference to serious medical needs of prisoners constitutes the 'unnecessary and wanton infliction of pain,'... proscribed by the Eighth amendment," said the Court, raising the possibility of pain and suffering that can amount to cruel and unusual punishment.[41] In like manner, involuntarily confined mentally disabled patients have a right to safe conditions, including food, shelter, and medical care, as well as minimally adequate training to avoid placement in physical restraints, as part of their substantive liberty interests guaranteed by the Due Process Clause of the Fourteenth Amendment.[42]

Federal Power to Provide for and Fund Health Care Programs

While the Constitution and Supreme Court interpretations do not identify a constitutional right to health care at the government's expense, Congress has enacted numerous statutes which establish and define specific statutory rights of individuals to receive medical services from the government. In addition, other statutes such as Title VI of the Civil Rights Act of 1964,[43] which prohibits discrimination under federally funded programs, affect the manner of delivery of services under federal grants and programs. As a major component of many health care entitlement statutes, Congress has provided funding to pay for the health care services offered under law. Most of these statutes have been enacted pursuant to Congress's authority to "make all Laws which shall be necessary and proper" to carry out its mandate "to ... provide for ... the general Welfare."[44]

Recently, Congress enacted comprehensive health care reform legislation, the Patient Protection and Affordable Care Act, P.L. 111-148. This statute imposes new requirements on individuals, employers, and the private health insurance market, and expands the Medicaid program, among other provisions. In doing so, Congress used its power to regulate interstate commerce, as well as its power to tax and spend for the general welfare.

The Taxing and Spending Power

The most frequently utilized grant of power in the Constitution for health care spending is that found in Article I, § 8, cl.1, which states in part that "[t]he Congress shall have Power to lay and collect Taxes, ... to ... provide for the ... general Welfare of the United States."[45] The last paragraph of this section provides that Congress shall have the authority "to make all Laws which shall be necessary and proper for carrying into Execution the foregoing Powers." The "foregoing Powers" include this specific power, popularly known as the taxing and spending power. Other powers in § 8 for which Congress has the authority to enact "necessary and proper" laws include Congress's power to provide for the common defense (cl. 1), to pay the debts of the United States (cl. 1), to borrow money (cl. 2), to regulate interstate commerce (cl. 3), to set citizenship requirements (cl. 4), to coin money (cl. 5), and to declare war (cl. 11).

The Supreme Court has recognized that Congress's power to tax is extremely broad. In *United States v. Doremus*, the Court stated that "[i]f the legislation enacted has some reasonable relation to the exercise of the taxing authority conferred by the Constitution, it cannot be invalidated because of the supposed motives which induced it."[46] In like manner, the power to spend for the general welfare is one of the broadest grants of authority to Congress in the United States Constitution.

The scope of the national spending power was brought before the United States Supreme Court in a landmark case in 1937 dealing with the newly enacted Social Security Act.[47] In *Steward Machine Co. v. Davis*,[48] the Court sustained a tax imposed on employers to provide unemployment benefits to individual workers. It was argued that the tax and a state credit that went with the state's tax were "weapons of coercion, destroying or impairing the autonomy of the States."[49] The Supreme Court, however, held that relief of unemployment was a legitimate object of federal spending under the "general welfare" clause, and that the Social Security Act, which also included old age benefits for individuals so they might not be destitute in their old age,[50] as well as provisions for child welfare and maternal child health projects, was a legitimate attempt to solve these problems in cooperation with the states.[51]

Subsequent Supreme Court decisions have not questioned Congress's policy decisions as to what kinds of spending programs are in pursuit of the "general welfare," and so numerous programs have been funded in such diverse areas as education, housing, veterans' benefits, the environment, welfare, health care, scientific research, the arts, community development, and public financing of election campaigns. The Supreme Court accords great deference to a legislative decision by Congress that a particular spending program provides for the general welfare. Indeed, the High Court has suggested that the question whether a spending program provides for the general welfare is one that is entirely within the discretion of the legislative branch. Thus, in *Buckley v. Valeo*,[52] the Supreme Court held that federal funding of election campaigns was a proper exercise of Congress's power to spend for the general welfare:[53]

> Appellants' "general welfare" contention erroneously treats the General Welfare Clause as a limitation upon congressional power. It is rather a grant of power, the scope of which is quite expansive, particularly in view of the enlargement of power by the Necessary and Proper Clause.... It is for Congress to decide which expenditures will promote the general welfare.... In this case, Congress was legislating for the "general welfare"—to reduce the deleterious influence of large contributions on our political process, to facilitate communication by candidates with the electorate, and to free candidates from the rigors of fundraising.... Whether the chosen means appear "bad," "unwise," or "unworkable" to us is irrelevant; Congress has concluded that the means are "necessary and proper" to promote the general welfare, and we thus decline to find this legislation without the grant of power in Art. I, §8.

Federally Funded Health Care Programs

The Medicare program, established in Title XVIII of the Social Security Act in 1965,[54] is the largest health care program enacted by Congress pursuant to its power to tax and spend for the general welfare. Medicaid (Title XIX),[55] also enacted in 1965, and the Children's Health Insurance Program (CHIP) (Title XXI),[56] enacted in 1997, are examples of voluntary federal/state partnership programs providing health care benefits to certain low-income persons. The Supreme Court has not taken a case challenging these health care programs as an unconstitutional exercise of Congress's taxing and spending power, possibly because the law on this point was settled by its earlier 1937 decision, discussed above, upholding Title II (Old Age Benefits) and Title III (Unemployment Compensation) of the same act.

Another example of a health care program is the Hospital Survey and Construction Act[57] (Hill-Burton Act), enacted in 1946, which offers federal construction funds to hospitals, nursing homes, and other health facilities on the condition that the facilities provide a reasonable volume of services to indigent patients, and make their services available to all persons residing in the facility's area.[58] Congress has also created a statutory right to certain emergency services under the Emergency Medical Treatment and Active Labor Act (EMTALA).[59] EMTALA imposes a legal obligation on hospitals that participate in Medicare to provide screening, examination, and stabilization of emergency medical conditions and women in labor, prior to transferring them to another facility.[60]

In addition, Congress has provided for health care services in many other contexts, including access to health care services for uninsured and underinsured persons through tax incentives to non-profit organizations such as hospitals for providing charitable care,[61] and by grant programs that fund certain "safety net providers," such as community health centers, migrant health centers, and other health facilities that serve medically underserved populations.[62]

Requirements under the Patient Protection and Affordable Care Act (PPACA), Including the Individual Mandate to Purchase Health Insurance

On March 23, the President signed into law H.R. 3590, the Patient Protection and Affordable Care Act (PPACA), P.L. 111-148,[63] a comprehensive health care reform bill. PPACA, which will be fully implemented by 2014, will restructure the private health insurance market, particularly for individuals purchasing coverage on their own (who may qualify for premium credits) and small businesses, partly by supporting states' creation of "American Health Benefit Exchanges" through which eligible individuals and small businesses can access private insurers' plans. Considerable attention has been paid to Section 1501 of Title I of PPACA, which will impose a mandate for most individuals to have health insurance or to pay a penalty for noncompliance, beginning in 2014.[64] Under this provision, individuals will be required to maintain minimum essential coverage for themselves and their dependents. Those who do not will be required to pay a penalty for each month of noncompliance. Some individuals will be provided subsidies to help pay for their premiums and cost-sharing. Others would be exempt from the individual mandate.[65]

Beginning in 2014, or sooner at state option, nonelderly, non-pregnant individuals with income below 133% of the federal poverty level will be newly eligible for Medicaid. From 2014 to 2016, the federal government will cover 100% of the Medicaid costs of these newly eligible individuals, with the percentage dropping to 90% (with states covering the difference) by 2020. This change represents the most significant expansion of Medicaid eligibility in many years. In addition, the health reform law adds new mandatory benefits to Medicaid, including, for example, coverage of services in free-standing birthing centers and tobacco cessation services for pregnant women. The new law also expands state options for providing home- and community-based services as an alternative to institutional care, and provides financial incentives to states to do so. Among the Medicaid financing changes, the health reform law reduces Medicaid disproportionate share hospital allotments, increases certain pharmacy reimbursements, increases primary care physician payment rates for selected preventive services, and increases federal spending for the territories.[66]

Lawsuits Challenging the Constitutionality of the Individual Health Insurance Mandate and Expansion of the Medicaid Program under PPACA

Several lawsuits have been filed in various federal courts challenging the constitutionality of the individual health insurance mandate and expansion of the Medicaid program under PPACA. On March 23, 2010, 13 states filed a lawsuit in Florida contending "[t]he Act represents an unprecedented encroachment on the liberty of individuals living in the Plaintiffs' respective states, by mandating that all citizens and legal residents of the United States have qualifying health care coverage or pay a tax penalty.... By imposing such a mandate, the Act exceeds the powers of the United States under Article I of the Constitution and violates the Tenth Amendment to the Constitution."[67] Several other states, certain individuals, and the National Federation of Independent Business have since joined in the lawsuit, *Florida v. U. S. Department of Health and Human Services,* bringing the total number of participating states to 20.[68] This lawsuit also contends that the financial burdens imposed on the states by the legislation's expansion of Medicaid "commandeers" states to devote their financial resources to achieve federal aims, thereby violating the Tenth Amendment to the Constitution. The states contend that the only alternative to spending billions more would be to drop out of the program, leaving millions of current Medicaid beneficiaries without health care coverage.[69]

On October 14, 2010, Judge Roger Vinson, in the *Florida* lawsuit, dismissed four of the six claims brought by the 20 states challenging PPACA.[70] The two remaining claims involve the challenge to the individual mandate as an exercise of Congress's constitutional authority to regulate interstate commerce and make laws "necessary and proper" for carrying out its powers, and the claim that expansion of the Medicaid program under the law is coercive. With regard to the individual mandate requirement, Judge Vinson stated that in order for the penalty for non-compliance "to be sustained, it must be sustained as a penalty imposed in aid of an enumerated power, to wit, the Commerce Clause power." In declining to dismiss the states' claim that expansion of the Medicaid program under the law is coercive, the judge noted that "the coercion theory has been often discussed in case law and scholarship, but (has) never actually (been) applied." However, the judge cited the Supreme Court's discussion of the possibility of coercion in *South Dakota v. Dole,* 483 U.S. 203 (1987), noting that "there is a line somewhere between mere pressure and impermissible coercion." Judge Vinson heard arguments on the merits of this case on December 14, 2010. The court is expected to issue a decision in early 2011.

A separate lawsuit, *Virginia v. Sebelius,* was filed by Virginia on the same day as the *Florida* lawsuit.[71] This lawsuit also challenges the individual health insurance mandate, but within the context of a recent Virginia law, discussed below, which arguably is inconsistent with the federal individual health insurance mandate, by stating that no resident of Virginia "shall be required to obtain or maintain a policy of individual insurance coverage."[72] On August 2, 2010, District Court Judge Henry E. Hudson denied HHS and the Department of Justice's motion to dismiss the lawsuit, allowing the case to move forward.[73] On December 13, 2011, Judge Hudson ruled that the requirement in Section 1501 of PPACA that individuals purchase health insurance is unconstitutional because it exceeds Congress's authority under the Commerce Clause.[74] The court explained that in order for a statute to survive a constitutional challenge under the Commerce Clause, it must, among other things, involve a self-initiated activity. Requiring the advance purchase of insurance based on a future need for health care services, the court found, is not an activity supported by Commerce Clause jurisprudence.[75] This decision is being appealed by the federal government.

A third lawsuit, *Thomas More Law Center v. Obama,* was filed by the Thomas More Law Center, a national public interest law firm, on behalf of itself and four individuals, alleging that "Congress lacks authority under the Commerce Clause of the Constitution to force private citizens, including Plaintiffs, under penalty of Federal law, to purchase health care coverage."[76] On October 7, Judge George Caram Steeh of the U.S. District Court for the Eastern District of Michigan, Southern Division, issued an order denying a motion for a preliminary injunction from the Thomas More Law Center and individual plaintiffs.[77] The court found that the federal requirement to purchase health insurance, "which addresses economic decisions regarding health care services that everybody eventually, and inevitably, will need, is a reasonable means of effectuating Congress' goal."[78] In another case, *Liberty University v. Geithner,*[143] the U.S. District Court for the Western District of Virginia employed similar reasoning in dismissing a lawsuit brought by a private Christian university and others. Both of these cases have been appealed to the circuit courts.

Other lawsuits have also been filed in various district courts and are awaiting judicial action; at least two such cases have been dismissed on procedural grounds.[79] It is expected that one or more of these cases may reach the Supreme Court. For a comprehensive analysis of the various constitutional issues raised by the individual requirement to purchase health insurance in Section 1501 of PPACA, see CRS Report R40725, *Requiring Individuals to Obtain Health Insurance: A Constitutional Analysis*, by Jennifer Staman et al.

State Attempts to "Nullify" or "Opt Out" of Federal Health Care Reform Requirements

On March 10, 2010, Virginia became the first state in the nation to enact a statute which states that, as a matter of law in Virginia, no individual (with certain exceptions) "shall be required to obtain or maintain a policy of individual insurance coverage," except as required by a court or state agency.[80] This state statute, entitled the Virginia Health Care Freedom Act, is arguably inconsistent with Section 1501 of PPACA, which requires individuals to purchase health insurance coverage beginning in 2014. While Virginia was the first state to pass a law relating to the federal requirement to purchase health insurance, legislators in at least 40 state legislatures have introduced bills to limit, change, or oppose various federal actions relating to health care reform, including the mandate to purchase health insurance or implementation of a single payer system.[81] Most measures seek to make or keep health insurance optional for individuals, and to ensure that individuals can purchase any kind of coverage they want. A Utah bill, signed into law on March 22, 2010, prohibits an individual health insurance mandate, and, in addition, prohibits any state agency from implementing federal health reform measures without the Utah legislature "specifically authorizing the state's compliance or participation in, federal health care reform."[82] As of the end of 2010, state statutes have been enacted in Virginia, Idaho, Utah, Georgia, Louisiana, Missouri, and Arizona that appear to exempt state residents from compliance with certain federal health care reform provisions in PPACA..

Some proposed state measures to opt out of, or limit, federal health reform measures have been in the form of state constitutional amendments which must be approved by a ballot vote. For example, the resolution passed by the Arizona legislature, and approved by Arizona voters on November 2, 2010, amended the Arizona state constitution to provide that "a law or rule shall not compel any person, employer or health care provider to participate in any health care system,..."[83] A similar state constitutional amendment providing in part that a "person or employer may pay directly for lawful health care services and shall not be required to pay penalties or fines for accepting direct payment from a person or employer for lawful health care services," was approved by voters in Oklahoma on November 2, 2010.[84] However, Colorado voters disapproved a similar ballot measure on the same date.[85]

A direct conflict between federal and state laws would raise constitutional issues which are likely to be resolved in favor of federal law under the Supremacy Clause of the Constitution, which states: "This Constitution, and the Laws of the United States which shall be made in Pursuance thereof; ... shall be the supreme Law of the Land; ... any Thing in the constitution or Laws of any State to the

Contrary notwithstanding."[86] When Congress legislates pursuant to its delegated powers, state laws, and even state constitutional provisions, must yield. For example, in *Cooper v. Aaron*, 358 U.S. 1 (1958), the U.S. Supreme Court upheld the federal law mandating desegregation of public schools in the face of Arkansas's constitutional amendment which prohibited integration.[87]

STATE CONSTITUTIONS AND THE PROVISION OF HEALTH CARE SERVICES

On the state level, governmental obligations to provide health care services either generally or for particular groups of persons may be found in a number of state constitutions. Thirteen state constitutions contain provisions which specifically refer to health.[88] The constitutions of the states of Alaska, Hawaii, Michigan, North Carolina, New York, and Wyoming have provisions which require the state to promote and protect the public health.[89] For example, Alaska's constitution provides that "[t]he legislature shall provide for the promotion and protection of public health."[90] And Wyoming's constitution states, "As the health and morality of the people are essential to their well-being, ... it shall be the duty of the legislature to protect and promote these vital interests."[91] Other state constitutional provisions permit, and sometimes require, legislative action to fund health care services for specific activities or for certain groups, such as indigent persons. Mississippi has a constitutional provision that authorizes laws for the care of the indigent sick in state hospitals.[92] Arkansas's constitution has a provision requiring the legislature to provide for the treatment of the insane.[93] By and large, however, state constitutional provisions authorize, but do not require, the provision of health care services.[94]

Some state courts have liberally construed state constitutional provisions mandating care of the poor to include the provision of health care services. For example, in *Graham v. Reserve Life Ins. Co.*,[95] a provision in the North Carolina constitution mandating "beneficent provision for the poor" was held to require state provision of free medical treatment to indigent sick persons. And the constitutionality of Alabama's Health Care Responsibility Act,[96] which imposed financial responsibility for the medical care of county indigents on counties, was upheld in part on the basis of Alabama's constitutional provision requiring counties "to make adequate provisions for the maintenance of the poor."[97] As a general matter, state constitutional rights may be more expansive than those found under the federal Bill of Rights, since federal rights set the minimum standards for the states. States are always free to provide for greater protections for their citizens than are provided on the national level.[98]

End Notes

[1] See Lawrence O. Gostin, "Securing Health or Just Health Care? The Effect of the Health Care System on the Health of America," 39 St. Louis U. L.J. 7 (1994), and Lawrence O. Gostin, "The Right to Health: A Right to the Highest Attainable Standard of Health, 31 HASTINGS CENTER REPORT 29-10 (2001).

[2] Constitution of the World Health Organization (2006), available at http://www.who.int/governance who_constitution_en.pdf.

[3] Health Insurance Portability and Accountability Act (HIPAA) Privacy Rule, 45 C.F.R. § 160.103.

[4] This report does not analyze the scope of a right to health or health care under various international agreements or under the governing documents of other countries. For further information see, for example, Puneet K. Sandhu, "A Legal Right to Health Care: What Can the United States Learn From Foreign Models of Health Rights Jurisprudence?" 95 Cal. L. Rev. 1151 (2007); and Marcela X. Berdion, "The Right to Health Care in the United States: Local Answers to Global Responsibilities," 60 SMU Law Review 1633 (2007).

[5] W. Kent Davis, "Answering Justice Ginsburg's Charge that the Constitution is 'Skimpy' in Comparison to our International Neighbors: A Comparison of Fundamental Rights in American and Foreign Law," 39 S. Tex. L. Rev. 951, 958 (1998).

[6] Id. at 958-959.

[7] 12 Pub. Papers 41 (Jan. 11, 1944).

[8] See *Roe v. Wade*, 410 U.S. 113 (1973) (constitutionally protected right to choose whether or not to terminate a pregnancy), and *Cruzan v. Missouri Department of Health*, 497 U.S. 261 (1990) (constitutional right to refuse medical treatment that sustains life), both of which involve a right to bodily integrity that may be extended to a person seeking health care services at his or her own expense.

[9] See, generally, discussion regarding fundamental rights in CRS, United States Constitution: Analysis and Interpretation, by Kenneth R. Thomas, p. 1763 et seq.

[10] See *San Antonio Indep. Sch. Dist. V. Rodriguez*, 411 U.S. 1, 33-35 (1973).

[11] *Griswold v. Connecticut*, 381 U.S. 479 (1965).

[12] *Skinner v. Oklahoma ex rel.* Williamson, 316 U.S. 535, 541 (1942).

[13] See *Griswold v. Connecticut*, 381 U.S. 479, 485 (1965).

[14] See *Roe v. Wade*, 410 U.S. 113, 153 (1973).

[15] See *Washington v. Harper*, 494 U.S. 210, 221-22 (1990) and *Winston v. Lee*, 470 U.S. 753, 766-67 (1985).

[16] It is noted that the Supreme Court has struck down state durational residence requirements for government benefits including health care services, but the constitutional right implicated was the right to travel, not a right to health care. See *Memorial Hospital v. Maricopa Cty.*, 415 U.S. 250, 269 (1974), where Arizona's one-year residency requirement for free medical care to indigents was held to violate equal protection guarantees and the right to travel.

[17] 432 U.S. 464 (1977).

[18] *Id.* at 473-474.

[19] 448 U.S. 297 (1980).

[20] Id. at 324.

[21] Id. at 318.

[22] Id.

[23] See *Webster v. Reproductive Health Servs.*, 492 U.S. 490, 507 (1989), where the Court noted that the "Due Process Clause generally confers no affirmative right to governmental aid, even when such aid may be necessary to secure life, liberty, or property interests."

[24] *Maher v. Roe*, 432 U.S. 464, 469 (1977). See, also, *Youngberg v. Romeo*, 457 U.S. 307, 317 (1982) ("[A] State is under no constitutional duty to provide substantive services for those within its borders.")

[25] See *Lindsey v. Normet*, 405 U.S. 56, 74 (1972), where the Supreme Court held that housing was not a fundamental constitutional right.

[26] See *San Antonio School District v. Rodriguez*, 411 U.S. 1, 37 (1973), where the Supreme Court acknowledged the importance of public education but refused to accord it the status of a fundamental constitutional right.

[27] 397 U.S. 254 (1970).

[28] Id. at 264-65.

[29] See also *Jefferson v. Hackney*, 406 U.S. 535, 546-48 (1972); *Dandridge v. Williams*, 397 U.S. 471, 486-87 (1970).

[30] *Harris v. McRae*, 448 U.S. at 322.

[31] See *Adarand Constructors, Inc. v. Pena*, 515 U.S. 200, 227 (1995); *McLaughlin v. Fla.*, 379 U.S. 184, 192 (1964).

[32] See Regents of *Univ. of Cal. v. Bakke*, 438 U.S. 265, 290-91 (1978).

[33] See *Oyama v. Cal.*, 332 U.S. 633, 646 (1948); see, also, *Korematsu v. United States*, 323 U.S. 214, 216 (1944).

[34] The Court has acknowledged that "laws and regulations allocating welfare funds involve 'the most basic economic needs of impoverished human beings,'" but still has upheld classifications based on wealth where the government can show a reasonable basis for the distinctions. Maher, 432 U.S. at 479, quoting *Dandridge v. Williams*, 397 U.S. 471, 485 (1970).

[35] 397 U.S. 471 (1970).

[36] Id. at 485.

[37] Id. at 487.

[38] For example, *United States v. Kras*, 409 U.S. 434 (1973); *Maher v. Roe*, 432 U.S. 464, 469 (1977); *Harris v. McRae*, 448 U.S. 297, 324 (1980).

[39] William P. Gunnar, "The Fundamental Law That Shapes the United States Health Care System: Is Universal Health Care Realistic Within the Established Paradigm?" 15 Annals Health L. 151, 164 (2006).

[40] *Farmer v. Brennan*, 511 U.S. 825, 832 (1994).

[41] *Estelle v. Gamble*, 429 U.S. 97, 104 (1976) (citing *Gregg v. Georgia*, 428 U.S. 153, 173 (1976)). See also *West v. Atkins*, 487 U.S. 42, 56 (1988): "Contracting out prison medical care does not relieve the State of its constitutional duty to provide adequate medical treatment to those in its custody, and it does not deprive the State's prisoners of the means to vindicate their Eighth Amendment rights."

[42] *Youngberg v. Romeo*, 457 U.S. 307, 315 (1982). By statute, Congress has mandated medical care for persons under a federal quarantine or isolation order, another example of the provision of medical care for persons with limited freedoms. 42 U.S.C. § 249(a).

[43] 42 U.S.C. §2000d. Specifically under Title VI, "[n]o person in the United States shall, on the ground of race, color, or national origin, be excluded from participation in, be denied the benefits of, or be subjected to discrimination under any program or activity receiving federal financial assistance." It has been suggested that Title VI "arguably was highly effective at

eliminating segregation among physicians in hospitals, ending high prepayment requirements for black patients, and eliminating discriminatory routing of ambulances." *(footnote omitted)* (Jennifer Gores, ed., "Health Care Law: Health Care Access," 8 Geo. J. Gender & L. 837, 842 (2007)).

[44] U.S. CONST. Art. I, § 8, cl. 18 and cl. 3. Congress also has the power to regulate health care under its power to regulate interstate commerce, and has done so when it has directly regulated the health care industry. Examples include the Employee Retirement Income Security Act of 1974 (ERISA) which regulates employee benefits, including health insurance, 29 U.S.C. 1001 *et seq.*; the Consolidated Omnibus Budget Reconciliation Act of 1986 (COBRA), which provides for insurance continuation requirements for certain persons who lose employment-related health insurance benefits, 29 U.S.C. §§ 1161-1168; various health insurance plan mandates for childbirth delivery hospital stays, breast reconstruction payments for mastectomies, and certain mental health coverage annual and life-time limit requirements, 29 U.S.C. §§ 1185, 1185a, 1185b; and, most recently, an individual mandate, for most Americans, to have health insurance coverage, which begins in 2014, Section 1501 of P.L. 111-148.

[45] It is noted that the Tenth Amendment provides that "powers not delegated to the United States by the Constitution, nor prohibited by it to the States, are reserved to the States respectively, or to the people." While this language would appear to represent one of the most clear examples of a federalist principle in the Constitution, it has not had a significant impact in limiting federal powers. See, for a general discussion of constitutional federalism principles, CRS Report RL30315, *Federalism, State Sovereignty, and the Constitution: Basis and Limits of Congressional Power*, by Kenneth R. Thomas.

[46] 249 U.S. 86, 93 (1919). For a discussion of certain limitations that do apply to Congress's power to tax, see, generally, CRS, *United States Constitution: Analysis and Interpretation*, coordinated by Kenneth R. Thomas, at http://www.crs.gov/conan/default.aspx?mode= topic&doc= Article01.xml&t=1|1&s=8&c=1.

[47] 42 U.S.C. 401 *et seq.*

[48] 301 U.S. 548 (1937).

[49] Id. at 591.

[50] See *Helvering v. Davis*, 301 U.S. 619 (1937), which upheld the old-age benefits provisions of Title II of the Social Security Act.

[51] *Steward Machine Co. v. Davis*, 301 U.S. 548, 591 (1937). The Supreme Court has suggested that there are limits to Congress's power under the Spending Clause to require states to meet grant conditions. For more information See CRS Report RL30315, *Federalism, State Sovereignty, and the Constitution: Basis and Limits of Congressional Power*, by Kenneth R. Thomas.

[52] 424 U.S. 1 (1975).

[53] Id. at 90-91.

[54] Medicare is a health insurance program for persons aged 65 and older, and certain other groups of persons such as persons with disabilities, and persons living with end-stage renal disease. 42 U.S.C. § 1395 *et seq.* For more information on the Medicare program See CRS Report R40425, *Medicare Primer*, coordinated by Patricia A. Davis.

[55] Medicaid is a need-based program that provides low-income persons with broad coverage for medical services. 42 U.S.C. § 1396 *et seq.* The states may participate in this voluntary grant program by submitting a state plan meeting federal requirements to the Department of Health and Human Services. 42 U.S.C. § 1396a(b). The federal government and the states jointly share the costs of providing benefits under this program. See CRS Report RL32950, *Medicaid: The Federal Medical Assistance Percentage (FMAP)*, by Evelyne P. Baumrucker.

[56] CHIP is a federal matching block grant program that provides health care services for certain uninsured children without access to Medicaid. 42 U.S.C. § 1397 *et seq.* See, for more information, CRS Report R40444, *State Children's Health Insurance Program (CHIP): A Brief Overview*, by Elicia J. Herz and Evelyne P. Baumrucker.

[57] 42 U.S.C. §§ 291 to 291o-1.

[58] See HHS website on the Hill-Burton Act at http://www.hrsa.gov/hillburton/default.htm.

[59] 42 U.S.C. §1395dd and regulations at 42 C.F.R. § 489.24. For more information on EMTALA, See CRS Report RS22738, *EMTALA: Access to Emergency Medical Care*, by Edward C. Liu.

[60] 42 U.S.C. § 1395dd(a)-(c).

[61] See 26 U.S.C. § 501(c)(3), which provides for an exemption from federal income tax of corporations organized and operated exclusively for religious, charitable, or educational purposes, provided not part of the organization's net earnings inures to the benefit of any private shareholder or individual. Under Rev. Rul. 69-545, 1969-2 C.B. 117, the IRS recognized "promotion of health" as a charitable purpose when a "community benefit" standard is met. See CRS Report RL34605, *501(c)(3) Hospitals and the Community Benefit Standard*, by Erika K. Lunder and Edward C. Liu.

[62] See CRS Report RL32046, *Federal Health Centers Program*, by Barbara English.

[63] It is noted that, on March 21, 2010, the House passed H.R. 4872, the Health Care and Education Reconciliation Act of 2010, P.L. 111-152, which made amendments to PPACA.

[64] Section 1501 of P.L. 111-148.

[65] Exempt individuals include those with qualifying religious exemptions, those in a health care sharing ministry, individuals not lawfully present in the United States, and incarcerated individuals. No penalty will be imposed on those without coverage for less than 90 days (with only one period of 90 days allowed in a year), members of Indian tribes, individuals whose household income does not exceed 100% of the federal poverty level (FPL), or any individual who the Secretary of HHS determines to have suffered a hardship with respect to the capability to obtain coverage under a qualified health plan. For more information about this, and related, provisions, CRS Report R40942, *Private Health Insurance Provisions in the Patient Protection and Affordable Care Act (PPACA)*, by Hinda Chaikind, Bernadette Fernandez, and Mark Newsom.

[66] For more information on the Medicaid provisions in PPACA, see CRS Report R41210, *Medicaid and the State Children's Health Insurance Program (CHIP) Provisions in PPACA: Summary and Timeline*, coordinated by Julie Stone.

[67] *Florida v. U.S. Department of Health and Human Services*, No. 3:10-cv-00091-RV-EMT, U.S. District Court for the Northern District of Florida (Pensacola). The original complaint (in which the following states joined Florida: AL, CO, ID, LA, MI, NE, PA, SC, SD, TX, UT, WA) is available at http://myfloridalegal.com/webfiles.nsf/WF/MRAY83TKWB/$file/HealthCareReformLawsuit.pdf.

[68] The additional states are AK, IN, ND, MS, NV, AZ, and GA. The amended complaint may be found at http://myfloridalegal.com/webfiles.nsf/WF/JFAO-85FNM9/$file/Complaint.pdf. Additional information about this lawsuit may be found at http://www.healthcarelawsuit.us/.

[69] It is noted that, even though it may be difficult as a practical matter for states to drop out, there is no requirement for states to participate in the Medicaid program. In addition, the Supreme Court has long upheld spending power programs, like Medicaid, that require states to comply with federal program requirements. See, for example, *South Dakota v. Dole*, 483 U.S. 203 (1987).

[70] Judge Vinson's court order in *Florida v. U.S. Department of Health and Human Services* may be viewed at http://myfloridalegal.com/webfiles.nsf/WF/CRUE-8A8REM/$file/Order+on+ MTD+ %5BDE+79%5D.pdf.

[71] Virginia *ex rel. Cuccinelli v. Sebelius*, No. 3:10cv188, U.S. District Court for the Eastern District of Virginia (Richmond), complaint available at http://www.vaag.com/ PRESS_ RELEASES/Cuccinelli/ Comm%20v.%20Sebelius%20-%20Complaint%20filed%20with%20 Court%20_323_10.pdf.

[72] See, discussion, supra, "State Attempts to "Nullify" or "Opt Out" of Federal Health Care Reform Requirements," and footnote 80. Ordinarily, federal law preempts state law; however, this lawsuit alleges that the Virginia statute should prevail because the federal law's mandate to purchase health insurance is unconstitutional.

[73] The judge's memorandum opinion may be viewed at http://www.vaag.virginia.gov/ PRESS_ RELEASES/Cuccinelli/Health%20Care%20Ruling.pdf.

[74] See *Virginia ex rel. Cuccinelli v. Sebelius,* No. 3:10cv188-HEH, slip opinion, available at http://documents.nytimes.com/health

[75] Id. at 23.

[76] *Thomas More Law Center v. Obama*, 2:10-cv-11156-GCS-RSW, U.S. District Court for the Eastern District of Michigan, complaint available at http://www.thomasmore.org/downloads/ sb_thomasmore/ TMLCFilesCourtChallengeMomentsAfterObamaHealt.pdf.

[77] *Thomas More Law Ctr. v. Obama,* 2010 U.S. Dist. LEXIS 107416 (Oct. 7, 2010). Judge Steeh's court order may be found at http://www.thomasmore.org/downloads/sbthomasmore/ Healthcare 10-07-10ORDERDENYINGPLAINTIFFSMOTIO.pdf.

[78] Id at 29.

[79] See, *New Jersey Physicians, Inc. v. Obama*, No. 10-1489 (NJ, filed Dec. 8, 2010); *Baldwin v. Sebelius*, No. 10-1033, (S.D. Cal., filed 8/27/10).

[80] Session Law, Chapter 106, available at http://leg6.state.va.us/cgi-bin/legp604.exe?101+ ful+CHAP0108+pdf, and codified at Virginia Code Section 38.2-3430.1:1.

[81] For a comprehensive and continually updated survey of state activity in this area, see National Conference of State Legislatures, "State Legislation Challenging Certain Health Reforms, 2010," at http://www.ncsl.org/default.aspx? tabid=18906.

[82] H.B. 67, enrolled copy available at http://le.utah.gov/~2010/bills/hbillenr/hb0067.pdf.

[83] See Arizona HCR 2014 of 2009, available at http://www.azleg.gov/legtext/ 49leg/1r/bills/ hcr2014h.pdf. In most states that provide for an amendment to the state's constitution by a ballot proposal, passage requires either a "supermajority" or two affirmative ballot votes in two separate years.

[84] Oklahoma Senate Joint Resolution 59 is available at https://www.sos.ok.gov/documents/questions/ 756.pdf.

[85] See National Conference of State Legislatures, "State Legislation Challenging Certain Health Reforms, 2010," at http://www.ncsl.org/default.aspx?tabid=18906.

[86] U.S. Const. Art. VI, cl. 2.

[87] See, also, *Gibbons v. Ogden*, 22 U.S. 9 Wheat. 11 (1824), *Douglas v. Seacoast Products, Inc*., 431 U.S. 265 (1977), and Timothy S. Jost, "Can the States Nullify Health Care Reform?" 362 New Eng. J. Med. 869-871 (March 11, 2010), available at http://content.nejm.org/cgi/content/full/ 362/10/869. For a general discussion of the Supremacy Clause, See CRS, *United States Constitution: Analysis and Interpretation,* coordinated by Kenneth R. Thomas, at http://www.crs.gov/conan/default.aspx?mode=topic&doc=Article06.xml&t=1|1&c=2.

[88] See, discussion and survey of state constitutional provisions relating to health care in article by Elizabeth Weeks Leonard, "State Constitutionalism and the Right to Health Care" (updated August 13, 2009), available at http://works.bepress.com/elizabeth_weeks/3/.

[89] See Rory Weiner, "Universal Health Insurance Under State Equal Protection Law," 23 W. New Eng. L. Rev. 327, 334 (2002).

[90] ALASKA CONST. art. VII, § 4 .

[91] WYO. CONST. art. 7, § 20.

[92] HAW. CONST. art. IX, § 3 and MISS. CONST. art. IV, § 86.

[93] ARK. CONST. art. 19, § 19.

[94] See, for example, the constitution of New York, which states that "[t]he protection and promotion of the health of the inhabitants of the state are matters of public concern and provision therefore shall be made by the state and by such of its subdivisions and in such manner, and by such means as the legislature shall from time to time determine." N. Y. CONST. art. 17, § 3. According to one author, state judicial decisions construing provisions of state constitutions "demonstrate a general reluctance to recognize affirmative, enforceable health rights." See, generally, Leonard, Part II.B, at 22-40, supra, footnote 88.

[95] 274 N.C. 115, 161 S.E.2d 485 (1968).

[96] ALA. CODE §§ 22-21-290 – 22-21-297.

[97] *Bd. of Comm'rs v. Bd. of Trs. of the Univ. of Ala.*, 483 So. 2d 1365, 1366 (Ala. Civ. App. 1985), and *Marengo County v. Univ. of S. Ala.*, 479 So. 2d 48, 51 (Ala. Civ. App. 1985). See also discussion generally at 333-337, Weiner, supra, footnote 89.

[98] See, for example, *Cruzan v. Dir., Mo. Dep't of Health*, 497 U.S. 261, 280-182 (1990), where the Court recognized that Missouri was entitled to accord stronger protection to preservation of life than federal law by requiring clear and convincing evidence to terminate life support.

In: Mandated Health Care: Constitutional Analysis ISBN: 978-1-61324-162-2
Editor: Jonathan P. Reilly © 2011 Nova Science Publishers, Inc.

Chapter 2

REQUIRING INDIVIDUALS TO OBTAIN HEALTH INSURANCE: A CONSTITUTIONAL ANALYSIS*

Jennifer Staman, Cynthia Brougher, Edward C. Liu, Erika K. Lunder and Kenneth R. Thomas

SUMMARY

As part of the Patient Protection and Affordable Care Act, P.L. 111-148, as amended, Congress enacted an "minimum essential coverage requirement," a provision compelling certain individuals to have a minimum level of health insurance (i.e., an "individual mandate"). Individuals who fail to do so are subject to a monetary penalty, administered through the tax code. Although the federal government provides health coverage for many individuals through federal programs such as Medicare, it had never before required individuals to purchase health insurance.

This report analyzes certain constitutional issues raised by compelling individuals to purchase health insurance. It addresses the authority of Congress to pass a law of this nature under its taxing power or its power to regulate interstate commerce. With regard to the taxing power, the requirement to purchase health insurance might be construed as a tax and

* This is an edited, reformatted and augmented version of a Congressional Research Services publication, dated December 16, 2010.

upheld so long as it was found to comply with the constitutional restrictions imposed on direct and indirect taxes. On the other hand, opponents of the minimum essential coverage requirement may argue that since it is imposed conditionally and may be avoided by compliance with regulations set out in the statute, that the requirement may be more accurately described as a penalty. If so, the taxing power alone might not provide Congress the constitutional authority to support this provision.

In evaluating under the minimum essential coverage requirement under the Commerce Clause, a court may rely on Supreme Court precedent and look to several factors to determine whether the minimum essential coverage requirement passes constitutional muster. Among other things, a court may evaluate whether the requirement is a regulation of economic activity. One could argue that the requirement to purchase health insurance is economic in nature because it regulates how an individual participates in the health care market, through insurance or otherwise. On the other hand, it may be argued that the minimum essential coverage requirement goes beyond the bounds of the clause, because while regulation of the health insurance industry or the health care system is economic activity, regulating a choice to purchase health insurance is not.

It has been questioned whether the requirement to have health insurance might violate certain protections found under the U.S. Constitution. This report discusses how a court might evaluate a challenge to the minimum essential coverage requirement on Fifth Amendment due process, takings clause, or equal protection grounds, as well as under the Tenth Amendment. This report also addresses whether the exceptions to the minimum essential coverage requirement to purchase health insurance satisfy First Amendment freedom of religion protections.

Several lawsuits have been filed that challenge the minimum essential coverage requirement on constitutional grounds. For example, in *Florida v. HHS*, attorneys general and governors in 20 states as well as others brought an action against the Secretaries of Health and Human Services, Treasury, and Labor, seeking declaratory and injunctive relief from certain provisions of PPACA. On October 14, 2010, the district court held that the claims against the minimum essential coverage requirement could proceed to the next stage of litigation. In *Virginia ex rel. Cuccinelli v. Sebelius,* the Virginia attorney general filed a separate lawsuit challenging the federal requirement to purchase health insurance. On December 13, 2010, the judge in the Virginia case found that the minimum essential coverage requirement is unconstitutional. In contrast, two federal district courts have upheld the minimum essential coverage requirement as a constitutional exercise of the Commerce Clause. Many expect that one or more of these cases will reach the Supreme Court.

INTRODUCTION

Although the federal government provides health coverage for many individuals through federal programs such as Medicare, it has never required individuals to purchase health insurance until the enactment of the Patient Protection and Affordable Care Act[1] (PPACA) in March of 2010.[2] While a requirement to transfer money to a private party may arise in other contexts (e.g., automobile insurance), it has been noted that these provisions are based on exercising a privilege, like driving a car.[3] Thus, due at least in part to the novelty of this requirement, questions over its constitutionality have been raised, and several lawsuits have challenged the minimum essential coverage requirement on constitutional grounds.

This report first analyzes the authority of Congress to enact the minimum essential coverage requirement contained in PPACA, as well as how a court might analyze this provision if challenged based on various provisions of the Fifth and Tenth Amendments. This report discusses whether there must be exceptions to a requirement to purchase health insurance based on First Amendment freedom of religion, and finally, discusses some of the legal challenges to this federal requirement.

BACKGROUND

Under Section 1501 of PPACA, beginning in tax year 2014, some taxpayers will be assessed a monetary penalty for any months during which they or their dependents lack "minimum essential" health coverage.[4] "Minimum essential coverage" includes coverage under a government-sponsored health care program (e.g., Medicaid, Part A of Medicare); an "eligible" employer-sponsored plan; coverage under a plan offered in the individual market; a grandfathered health plan; and other health coverage as recognized by the Secretary of Health and Human Services.

The amount of the assessment for failing to meet the minimum essential coverage requirement, which can be prorated for partial compliance during the year, is determined by taking the greater of a flat dollar amount and a calculation based on a percentage of the taxpayer's household income. The annual flat dollar amount is assessed per individual or dependent without coverage and will be phased in over three years. The amount is set at $95 for 2014; $325 for 2015; and

$695 in 2016 and thereafter.[5] This amount will also be adjusted for inflation beyond 2016.

Although this is a fixed per-person amount, a taxpayer's liability will not exceed three times this amount per year, regardless of the number of individuals who actually lack adequate coverage during the year. For example, a married couple filing jointly with two dependent children and no health insurance will have the same flat dollar assessment as a similarly situated married couple with three dependent children.

This flat dollar amount will be compared to a percentage of the extent to which the taxpayer's household income exceeds the income tax filing threshold.[6] Like the flat dollar amount, the applicable percentage to be used is phased in over three years, set at 1% for 2014, 2% for 2015, and 2.5% thereafter. The amount assessed on a taxpayer who lacks minimum essential coverage will be equal to the greater of the flat dollar amount or the calculated percentage of household income. However, this amount shall not exceed the national average of the annual premiums of a bronze level health insurance plan offered through an exchange created under PPACA.

Exemptions would apply to individuals with qualified religious exemptions, members of health care sharing ministries, unauthorized aliens, incarcerated individuals, qualified U.S. citizens and residents living abroad, and bona fide residents of the U.S. possessions. Additionally, no amounts would be assessed on individuals who could not afford coverage;[7] taxpayers with income less than the filing threshold; members of Indian tribes; and individuals granted hardship exceptions. Finally, no amounts would be assessed for periods without coverage that last less than three months. This three-month exception could apply to only one continuous period without coverage during a calendar year.

Constitutional Authority to Require an Individual to Have Health Insurance

In analyzing the constitutionality of PPACA's requirement to obtain health insurance, the first question is the congressional authority for this requirement based on Congress's enumerated powers. While there is no specific enumerated power to regulate health care or establish a minimum essential coverage requirement, one can look to Congress's other broad enumerated powers which have been used to justify social programs in the past. In the instant case, Congress's taxing power could be applicable. In addition, Congress's power to regulate interstate commerce may also be pertinent, especially given that Section 1501 of PPACA , as amended, provides numerous findings about the correlation or the minimum essential coverage requirement to interstate commerce.

Taxing Power

Article I, Section 8 of the Constitution states that "Congress shall have Power To lay and collect Taxes, Duties, Imposts and Excises, to pay the Debts and provide for the common Defence and general Welfare of the United States.... " The power to tax and spend for the general welfare is one of the broadest powers in the Constitution and affords the basis of government health programs in the Social Security Act, including Medicare, Medicaid, and the State Children's Health Insurance Program.

Because Congress's power to tax is extremely broad,[8] a court might look to it as a legitimate source of power for Congress to impose the minimum essential coverage requirement. If so, the provision might be upheld as constitutional so long as it was found to comply with the constitutional restrictions imposed on direct and indirect taxes discussed below. In such case, a court might favorably compare the requirement to other examples of where Congress has used its taxing authority to create financial incentives for individuals to purchase health insurance.[9] Similarly, if Congress were to require individuals to purchase health insurance, and then encourage compliance with this requirement by conditioning receipt of a tax benefit (e.g., a tax credit) on the purchase of health insurance, this incentive also could be seen as a legitimate exercise of Congress's taxing authority.

On the other hand, opponents of the minimum essential coverage requirement may note that the enacted requirement differs in that it creates a financial disincentive for failing to obtain health insurance. As the tax is imposed conditionally and may be avoided by compliance with regulations set out in the statute, some might argue that it may also be accurately described as a penalty and, therefore, the taxing power alone might not provide Congress the constitutional authority to impose the requirement.[10] A court analyzing this argument might look to cases where the Supreme Court has examined whether Congress has the authority, independent of its taxing authority, to regulate the underlying subject matter. If such regulation is authorized under a provision of the Constitution other than the taxing power, the exaction may be sustained as an appropriate enforcement mechanism.[11] But, in the absence of such independent authority, a tax triggered by the failure to comply with federal standards has been held to be invalid.[12]

A court that found it necessary to determine whether the character of the minimum essential coverage payment is that of a tax or penalty would likely examine congressional intent. The Court has noted that

> the difference between a tax and a penalty is sometimes difficult to define and yet the consequences of the distinction in the required method of their collection often are important.... Taxes are occasionally imposed in the discretion of the legislature on proper subjects with the *primary* motive of obtaining revenue from them and with the *incidental* motive of discouraging them by making their continuance onerous. They do not lose their character as taxes because of the incidental motive. But there comes a time in the extension of the penalizing features of the so-called tax when it loses its character as such and becomes a mere penalty with the characteristics of regulation and punishment.[13]

Here, enforcement of this provision would likely result in revenue for the federal government, and a court might find this to be a sufficient purpose to be a valid exercise of the taxing power. But, it may be difficult for a court to ignore the larger context of health insurance reform in which the provision has arisen. To the extent that this context indicates that a primary motive of the provision is to encourage compliance with a federal requirement that individuals maintain some form of health insurance, a court may characterize it as a penalty rather than a tax.

For example, a court might look to any legislative findings accompanying the minimum essential coverage requirement. Notably, Congress found that

> [t]he [minimum essential coverage] requirement regulates activity that is commercial and economic in nature: economic and financial decisions about how and when health care is paid for, and when health insurance is purchased.[14]

The language Congress itself uses to refer to the provision may also influence its characterization. On one hand, simply because Congress has labeled a provision as a tax, a court is not bound by that label.[15] However, neither would a court be prohibited from using Congress's description of the provision as a penalty as evidence of Congress's intent.

Other factors can be gleaned from the Court's jurisprudence distinguishing taxes and penalties. Factors which suggest that a provision might actually be a penalty include (1) the absence of a correlation between the amount of tax and the magnitude by which an individual's conduct deviates from the conduct which is exempt from taxation; (2) a limitation that the tax only fall on individuals that knowingly deviate from the exempt conduct; and (3) the possibility of enforcement by government entities not traditionally charged with the enforcement of taxes.[16]

Application of these three factors to the instant provision would appear to support its characterization as a tax. First, the amount of the penalty is roughly proportional to the length of time during the year that the taxpayer and his or her dependents lacked coverage. Second, knowledge is not a necessary element to assess the penalty. Third, it appears that the provision will be enforced by the Internal Revenue Service, an entity traditionally charged with the enforcement of taxes. However, this list comprises only those factors the Court found present in the case before it, and may not represent an exhaustive list of what a court might consider as indicia of taxes.

If a court were to classify the provision as a penalty, this would not be determinative of its constitutional validity, but would merely establish that Congress's authority to enact such a provision must be found in something other than its power to levy taxes. In other words, the constitutionality of the minimum essential coverage requirement, if determined to be a penalty, would depend upon whether Congress has the authority under a power other than the taxing power to impose a financial burden on individuals that lack health insurance. As discussed below, one potential source of such authority may be the Commerce Clause.

Limits on the Taxing Power

Even where Congress has the general authority to levy a tax, the Constitution may impose additional requirements on the form of such taxes. For constitutional purposes,[17] taxes are understood to be either

- direct taxes, subject to apportionment among the states based on population,[18] or
- indirect taxes (i.e., duties, imposts, and excises), subject to the Uniformity Clause.[19]

Additionally, under the Sixteenth Amendment, taxes on income, from whatever source, are not required to be apportioned,[20] even if such taxes are direct. The amendment itself does not classify income taxes as direct or indirect.

Here, it appears the minimum essential coverage requirement would raise constitutional concerns under these provisions only if it was found to be a direct tax that was not a tax on income. This is because it would then be subject to the requirement of apportionment, and there is no indication it will be apportioned among the states based on population. If, however, the requirement was found to be a tax on income, it would fall under the protection of the Sixteenth Amendment and its lack of apportionment would raise no constitutional concerns. Similarly, it appears no constitutional issues would arise if the requirement was found to be an indirect tax since it would appear to satisfy the requirement of uniformity since it is geographically neutral on its face.[21]

Some have argued that the minimum essential coverage requirement is in fact a direct tax, and, consequently, must be apportioned. The exact scope of the term "direct taxes" is undetermined, but the Court has construed it to be relatively narrow. The Constitution does not define the term other than specifying that it includes capitations (a capitation, or head tax, is a fixed tax imposed on each person in a jurisdiction). The Framers' debates provide little clarity.[22] From its earliest days, the Supreme Court has indicated that direct taxes include capitations and real property taxes at a minimum.[23] The Court has also suggested that other types of taxes might be considered direct,[24] although the Court did not find any such examples[25] until the *Pollock* case in 1895. In *Pollock*, the Court struck down the unapportioned Income Tax Act of 1894[26] after finding parts of it—the taxes on income from real and personal property—were direct taxes.[27] The *Pollock* decision was subject to substantial criticism and led to the adoption of the Sixteenth Amendment in 1913. *Pollock* has not been expressly overruled,[28] although the Court moved away from its analysis in subsequent cases that upheld a variety of unapportioned taxes on the basis they were excise taxes.[29]

The minimum essential coverage requirement is codified in the Internal Revenue Code as an excise tax. For constitutional purposes, the Supreme Court has found excise taxes to be a broad category of indirect taxes.[30] It might be argued, for example, that the tax is properly characterized as an excise tax imposed on earning income without maintaining health insurance for oneself and one's dependents.[31] Excise taxes imposed on inaction are not unprecedented,[32] although it does not appear that any have been challenged on the grounds that it is unconstitutional to impose an excise tax on a failure to act.

On the other hand, some have argued that the minimum essential coverage requirement is a tax based on inaction and is effectively a capitation.[33] Under this argument, "[a] tax on a person who chooses not to act is precariously close to a tax on everyone with an exemption from the tax for those that act."[34] In other words, a tax on the failure to act (i.e., buy health insurance) is essentially a tax on "the state of mere existence."[35] However, others might point to the fact that the tax would not be imposed on individuals with insufficient income as evidence that it should not be characterized as a capitation. Additionally, some might compare it to existing tax deductions and credits that are intended to encourage certain types of behaviors, such as the tax benefits provided to homeowners.[36] It might be argued that the minimum essential coverage requirement is analogous to these types of provisions, and the fact that it takes a different form (i.e., is not a deduction or credit) should not be constitutionally significant.

Resolving this point may require determining whether a generally applicable tax that is avoidable if an individual takes some action constitutes a capitation. The federal courts have yet to explore in detail the precise definition of capitations, also known as poll taxes, for purposes of the federal Constitution. However, some insight into their meanings may be gleaned from the states' attitudes regarding poll taxes which were held contemporaneously with the ratification of the federal constitution. For example, in *Short v. State* the Maryland Court of Appeals was confronted with the meaning of poll taxes for purposes of the state constitution. At the time of the case in 1895, every Maryland state constitution since 1776 had prohibited poll taxes.[37] Maryland had also required, at least since 1795, that all able-bodied state male residents either spend two days a year improving the road system or pay seventy-five cents for road maintenance. Based upon approximately one hundred years of coexistence between these two provisions, the Marylan Court of Appeals determined that the meaning of poll taxes, as used in the state constitution in 1776, did not encompass the financial penalty imposed on those who failed to perform road maintenance.[38] A potential inference from this holding is that, at the time the Constitution was drafted, the common understanding of poll taxes did not encompass a financial penalty imposed on the failure to satisfy a lawful obligation to take some action. Therefore, while Congress's authority to impose the underlying mandate may be challenged, it is far from certain that a tax on individuals who fail to comply with that mandate would be a capitation necessitating apportionment.

If the minimum essential coverage requirement is classified as a tax on income, whether the tax is direct or not becomes irrelevant as it would no longer be subject to apportionment by virtue of the Sixteenth Amendment. Certain aspects of the tax might support its classification as a tax on income since, for taxpayers with sufficient income, the amount of taxation would be directly proportional to their excess household income above the filing threshold and only those taxpayers with household income above the filing threshold would be subject to the tax at all. However, it is not clear that a court would classify the minimum essential coverage requirement as a tax on income since a significant component of the tax appears to have no relationship to a taxpayer's income, but is instead related to the lack of coverage under a health plan for themselves and their dependents.

Power to Regulate Commerce

The Commerce Clause of the U.S. Constitution empowers Congress "[t]o regulate Commerce with foreign Nations, and among the several States, and with the Indian Tribes."[39] The Supreme Court developed an expansive view of the Commerce Clause relatively early in the history of judicial review.[40] This power has been cited as the constitutional basis for a significant portion of the laws passed by the Congress over the last 50 years, and it currently represents one of the broadest bases for the exercise of congressional powers.[41] While the Supreme Court held in *United States v. South-Eastern Underwriters Association*[42] that Congress could regulate the competitive practices of insurers under the Commerce Clause, it is unclear whether the minimum essential coverage requirement could be considered regulation of insurance per se. Despite the breadth of powers that have been exercised under the Commerce Clause, whether the minimum essential coverage requirement would be constitutional under the clause is a challenging question, as it is a novel issue whether Congress may use the clause to require an individual to purchase a good or a service.

Under modern Commerce Clause jurisprudence, the Supreme Court has found that the Commerce Clause allows for three categories of congressional regulation: the channels of interstate commerce; the instrumentalities of interstate commerce; and "those activities having a substantial relation to interstate commerce ... i.e., those activities that substantially affect interstate commerce."[43] It is likely that a court would evaluate Congress's authority for enacting the minimum essential coverage requirement under this third "substantially affects" category.

Three recent cases, *United States v. Lopez, United States v. Morrison,*[44] *and Gonzales v. Raich,*[45] as well as several historical decisions such as *Wickard v. Filburn,*[46] govern much of the current Commerce Clause analysis under the "substantially affects" category. These cases indicate that, while the modern interpretation of the Commerce Clause is broad, congressional authority is not without bounds.[47] In a case that has been perceived as one of the Supreme Court's most expansive Commerce Clause rulings, *Wickard v. Filburn*, the Court was asked to determine whether the clause permitted amendments to the Agricultural Adjustment Act of 1938 affecting the production and consumption of homegrown wheat.[48] In upholding the statute as constitutional, the Court held that economic activities, regardless of their nature, could be regulated by Congress if the activity exerts a substantial effect on interstate commerce.[49] Although the Court admitted that one family's production alone would likely have a negligible impact on the overall price of wheat, if combined with other personal producers, the effect would be substantial enough to make the activity subject to congressional regulation.[50] The Court concluded that Congress had a rational basis for its action and its belief that, in the aggregate, keeping homegrown wheat outside of federal regulation would have a substantial influence on interstate commerce.

From 1937 to 1995, after cases like *Wickard* and others, the Supreme Court did not hold a federal statute to be beyond the scope of the authority vested in Congress by the Commerce Clause. However, in 1995, in *United States v. Lopez*, the Court struck down a statute that made it a federal crime to knowingly possess a firearm in a school zone because it exceeded Congress's Commerce Clause authority. In analyzing the statute under the "substantially affects" category, the Court identified four major problems. First, it determined that the criminal statute at issue had no connection with commerce or any sort of economic enterprise, and did not play an essential role in a larger regulatory scheme. Secondly, the Supreme Court found it significant that there was no jurisdictional element in the statute, which would ensure that firearm possession affected interstate commerce in a particular instance. Third, the Court stated that the lack of congressional findings regarding the impact of the offense on the national economy detracted from any substantial relation it might have to interstate commerce. Finally, the Court rejected the government's argument that the statute was valid because possession of a firearm near a school could result in violent crime, and this crime could affect the national economy. The Court explained that if it were to accept the government's arguments, it would be hard "to posit any activity by an individual that Congress is without power to regulate."[51]

The Supreme Court used the logic of *Lopez* in *United States v. Morrison*, where the Court evaluated whether a federal statute that provided for a private right of action for victims of gender-motivated violence fell within Congress's power under the Commerce Clause. In finding that this statute was beyond Congress's authority under the Commerce Clause, the Court followed the analysis in *Lopez*. First, the Court explained that "gender-motivated crimes are not, in any sense of the phrase, economic activity." Turning to the second prong of the *Lopez* analysis, the Court noted that, like the Gun-Free School Zones Act, the statute lacked a "jurisdictional element establishing that the federal cause of action is in pursuance of Congress' power to regulate interstate commerce."[52]

The Court then discussed the existence of congressional findings regarding the effects of gender-motivated violence on the national economy and interstate commerce. While noting that the statute was supported by "numerous findings,"[53] the Court stressed its declaration in *Lopez* that "[s]imply because Congress may conclude that a particular activity substantially affects interstate commerce does not necessarily make it so." Finally, the Court considered the level of attenuation between the federal statute and its effect on interstate commerce. In explaining why the statute exceeded the boundaries of the Commerce Clause, the Court explained that the statute would impermissibly provide Congress with the power "to regulate any crime as long as the nationwide, aggregated impact of that crime has substantial effects on employment, production, transit, or consumption."[54] Expanding upon this observation, the Court noted that to allow such regulation of a non-economic activity would enable federal regulation of almost any activity, including "family law and other areas of traditional state regulation.... "[55]

In *Gonzales v. Raich*, the Supreme Court evaluated whether, under the Commerce Clause, Congress had the power to apply the federal Controlled Substances Act's (CSA's) prohibition of the manufacture and possession of marijuana to the local cultivation and use of marijuana that was in compliance with California law. In holding that the CSA's prohibition was within Congress's authority under the Commerce Clause, the Court relied on *Wickard v. Filburn* and the idea that Congress can regulate purely intrastate activity that is not "commercial" if it concludes that failure to regulate the activity would undercut federal regulation of the interstate market.[56] However, the Court found that the standard for assessing the scope of Congress's power under the Commerce Clause is not whether the activity at issue, when aggregated, substantially affect interstate commerce; but rather, whether there exists a "rational basis" for Congress to have reached that conclusion. Further, the Court distinguished *Raich* from *Lopez* and *Morrison* based on the idea that in *Raich*, the regulated activity was "quintessentially economic."[57] The Court also concluded that Congress had acted rationally in determining that the CSA's prohibition of the class of activities at issue was an "an essential part of the larger regulation of economic activity."[58]

In applying the 4-factor analysis used in *Lopez* and *Morrison* to the minimum essential coverage requirement of PPACA,[59] the first and fourth factors of these cases warrant the closest analysis. Under the first factor of the test, it must be determined whether requiring individuals to purchase health insurance is commercial or economic in nature. In *Lopez*, the gun control law at issue was struck down by the Supreme Court, as was a cause of action based on gender-motivated crime in *Morrison*, because the statutes did not have anything to do with an economic activity or enterprise. While the regulation of the health insurance industry or the health care system would likely be considered economic in nature, a requirement to purchase health insurance is more of an open question. One could make the argument that the requirement to purchase health insurance is economic in nature because it essentially requires an individual to be a consumer in the health insurance market. In *Lopez*, the Court pointed out that the gun control law was not a regulation of activity that "arises out of or is connected with a commercial transaction" which viewed in the aggregate, substantially affects interstate commerce. A requirement to purchase health insurance could be seen as a commercial transaction, especially since the minimum essential coverage requirement can be fulfilled by purchasing insurance from a private insurance company.

On the other hand, it may be argued that the minimum essential coverage requirement goes beyond the bounds of the Commerce Clause. One could argue that while regulation of the health insurance industry or the health care system could be considered economic activity, regulating a choice to purchase health insurance is not. It may also be questioned whether a requirement to purchase health insurance is really a regulation of an economic activity or enterprise, if individuals who would be required to purchase health insurance are not, but for this regulation, a part of the health insurance market. In general, Congress has used its authority under the Commerce Clause to regulate individuals, employers, and others who voluntarily take part in some type of economic activity. While in *Wickard* and *Raich*, the individuals were participating in their own home activities (i.e., producing wheat for home consumption and cultivating marijuana for personal use), they were acting of their own volition, and this activity was determined to be economic in nature and affected interstate commerce. However, a requirement could be imposed on some individuals who do not engage in any economic activity relating to the health insurance market. This is a novel issue: whether Congress can use its Commerce Clause authority to require a person to buy a good or a service and whether this type of required participation can be considered economic activity. Still, while it may seem like too much of a bootstrap to force individuals into the health insurance market and then use their participation in that market to say they are engaging in commerce, there is plenty of evidence that the purchase of health insurance has an effect on the commerce of the nation. For example, in 2008, health care expenditures in the United States grew 4.4% to $2.3 trillion, or $7,681 per person, and accounted for 16.2% of gross domestic product.[60]

Perhaps one example of the regulation of voluntary individual behavior is the use of the Commerce Clause to prohibit criminal activity. While in *Lopez* and *Morrison* the Supreme Court found that the criminal statute exceeded Congress's Commerce Clause authority, courts have upheld other federal criminal statutes as acceptable under the Commerce Clause.[61] One notable case, *U.S. v. Bishop*, upheld congressional authority to enact a carjacking statute. In *Bishop*, the court, in *dicta,* briefly addressed the voluntariness factor, finding that commerce does not have to be a "voluntary economic exchange."[62] In addition, certain federal criminal statutes require a person to take action, and penalize that person for failure to take that action. For example, an individual who willfully fails to pay a child support obligation with respect to a child who resides in another state may be subject to criminal penalties, subject to certain requirements.[63] However, while criminal statutes evaluated under the Commerce Clause may provide some insight as to how a court would evaluate a requirement to purchase health insurance, these cases are not entirely instructive.

In evaluating whether the minimum essential coverage requirement and the effect on interstate commerce is attenuated, one may point to evidence of the effect that the requirement to purchase health insurance would have on the insurance industry and the health care system as a whole. One could argue that because most individuals do, at some point, become ill and require health care, a requirement that all persons purchase health insurance coverage would benefit the orderly flow of health care services in interstate commerce. As pointed out in the findings accompanying the minimum essential coverage requirement, the requirement regulates activity such as "the economic and financial decisions about how and when health care is paid for, and when health insurance is purchased. In the absence of the requirement, some individuals would make an economic and financial decision to forego health insurance coverage and attempt to self-insure, which increases financial risks to households and medical providers."[64] Also, because one of the motivating factors for a requirement to obtain health insurance may be to get healthy individuals who do not have health insurance to purchase it (so as to offset the cost of the individuals who need greater, more expensive care), this also would contribute to the proper functioning of the health care system. Still, one could argue that if the commerce power can be used to mandate the purchases of a private individual, it could be perceived as virtually unlimited in scope.[65] Based on similar arguments made in *Lopez* and *Morrison*, there may be questions raised about whether Congress can require the purchase of any good or service based on the effect such purchases could have on an industry or the economy as a whole.

Also, while perhaps not as important to the instant inquiry as the other *Lopez/Morrison* factors, a reviewing court may examine the presence of congressional findings for purposes of commerce clause analysis. PPACA includes detailed findings regarding the effect that the minimum essential coverage requirement would have on interstate commerce.[66] However, as mentioned above, it appears that the presence of congressional findings may be helpful, but not determinative, of Congress's authority to legislate under the Commerce Clause. In addition, as discussed in *Lopez* and *Morrison*, a reviewing court may also examine the fact that PPACA does not contain an explicit jurisdictional element that insures that the statute affects interstate commerce. This element could have been satisfied by a statement, such as one providing that any person using medical care in or affecting interstate commerce must have health insurance. It is possible that a court may overlook the need for a jurisdictional element, especially in light of Congress's findings that indicate the effects that the minimum essential coverage requirement has on interstate commerce.[67] However, should a reviewing court find that absence of a jurisdictional element as essential for Congress's ability to enact the minimum essential coverage requirement, it seems possible that Congress may be able to amend PPACA to include this element.[68]

Following the reasoning of *Raich*, a court may examine whether Congress rationally concluded that persons failing to have health insurance have a substantial effect on interstate commerce. One arguing in favor of the constitutionality of the minimum essential coverage requirement may point to the fact that a health insurance mandate would presumably lower the uninsured population. It has been suggested that Americans without health coverage burdens our health care system and adds strain on the economy.[69] As indicated in the congressional findings accompanying the minimum essential coverage requirement, the economy loses up to $207 billion a year because of the poorer health and shorter lifespan of the uninsured.[70] Further, according to these findings, in 2008, cost of providing uncompensated care to the uninsured was $43 billion and these amounts are paid for when health care providers pass on the cost to private insurers, which pass on the cost to those who are insured. Evidence like this could demonstrate a rational basis for Congress's enactment of a requirement to purchase health insurance.

In addition, based on *Raich*, if a requirement to purchase health insurance is not considered economic or commercial in nature, it should be determined whether the requirement is "an essential part of a larger regulation of economic activity." One may argue that a minimum essential coverage requirement, while not commercial in nature, is an essential part of Congress's current regulation of the health care system or industry. A reviewing court could consider whether the absence of a requirement to purchase health care would undercut the regulation of the health care as a whole. In making this determination, a court may look to the involvement of the federal government in the regulation of health care generally to decide whether a requirement to purchase health insurance could be seen as an essential component of this regulation. Given the federal government's fairly significant role in health care regulation (e.g., ERISA, the Public Health Service Act), the argument that the requirement to purchase insurance is an "essential part" of the regulation may become more viable. In addition, since the minimum essential coverage requirement is part of comprehensive act dealing with many aspects of health care, this may reinforce the idea that it is acceptable under the Commerce Clause as part of a larger health care reform effort.[71]

Further, it may be argued that the minimum essential coverage requirement plays an integral role within PPACA itself, because of certain new insurance requirements that require health insurers to accept every individual that applies for coverage, and prevent insurers from imposing exclusions from coverage based on preexisting conditions. One may argue that without a minimum essential coverage requirement, individuals could wait to purchase health insurance until they needed care. As congressional findings point out, "[t]he [minimum essential coverage] requirement is essential to creating effective health insurance markets in which improved health insurance products that are guaranteed issue and do not exclude coverage of pre-existing conditions can be sold."[72] On the other hand, one could point out that under Section 1501 of PPACA, an individual could decide to pay the penalty associated with the minimum essential coverage requirement and avoid purchasing health insurance. If there were to be large scale noncompliance with the requirement to purchase health insurance, this may weaken the idea that minimum essential coverage requirement is an essential part of this health care regulation.

Health Insurance Coverage Requirements and the Fifth and Tenth Amendments

Some commentators have questioned whether a requirement to have health insurance might violate certain protections found under the U.S. Constitution.[73] This section provides a general discussion of how a court might evaluate a health insurance requirement that is challenged on Fifth Amendment due process, takings clause, or equal protection grounds, as well as under the Tenth Amendment. In general, it seems unlikely that a challenge to the minimum essential coverage requirement would be successful under these provisions.

Substantive due Process

The Fifth Amendment states, in relevant part, that "[n]o person shall be ... deprived of life, liberty, or property, without due process of law.... "[74] The Supreme Court has understood due process to protect both procedural and substantive rights. Under the doctrine of substantive due process, the Court has held that certain fundamental rights, while not expressly recognized in the text of the Constitution, are subsumed within the notion of liberty in the Due Process Clause. If the Court determines that a right is fundamental, any government infringement of that right will be subject to strict scrutiny. Strict scrutiny is the most rigorous form of judicial review applied by a reviewing court, and government action will survive strict scrutiny only if such action is narrowly tailored to achieving a compelling government interest.[75] Where there is no fundamental right involved, the government must demonstrate that there is a rational basis for its action.[76] This level of judicial review, referred to as rational basis review, is characterized by its deference to legislative judgment. Because of the distinction between strict scrutiny and rational basis review, a determination of whether there is a fundamental right is central to a substantive due process analysis.

To date, the Supreme Court has not articulated a fundamental right to health care.[77] Indeed, the words "health" or "medical care" do not appear anywhere in the text of the Constitution. Thus, rights of individuals to health care services derive from statutory rights (with a few such rights also set forth in state constitutions) and have most often concerned the provision of medical care to poor persons. In challenging a health insurance mandate on due process grounds, it is possible that one could allege a fundamental right to be uninsured, or to not purchase health insurance.

However, this is not a fundamental right that has been recognized by the Supreme Court.[78] While the Supreme Court has recognized a constitutional right to privacy, and, arguably within that right, a right to be left alone (i.e., protection against "invasion of [one's] indefeasible right of personal security, personal liberty and private property"),[79] it does not seem that a requirement to make a purchase of health insurance would rise to the level of interference with this fundamental right. Thus, because there does not appear to be an imposition on any fundamental right that would trigger heightened scrutiny, the minimum essential coverage requirement would likely be evaluated under a rational basis review and upheld.

It is possible that a reviewing court would evaluate the requirement to purchase health insurance as economic legislation. In evaluating claims that economic regulations violate a person's rights under the Due Process clause, the Court has pronounced a strict "hands-off" standard of judicial review and implements a rational basis test.[80] As a "legislative Act" adjusting the burdens and benefits of economic life," such a law enjoys a strong "presumption of constitutionality," and the "burden is on one complaining of a due process violation to establish that the legislature has acted in an arbitrary and irrational way."[81] If the economic legislation "is supported by a legitimate legislative purpose furthered by rational means, judgments about the wisdom of such legislation remain within the exclusive province of the legislative and executive branches."[82] The Court has suggested that the accommodation among interests which the legislative branch has "struck may have profound and far-reaching consequences ... [and] provides all the more reason for this Court to defer to the congressional judgment unless it is demonstrably arbitrary or irrational."[83]

If a court were to view the minimum essential coverage requirement as economic legislation (i.e., a legislative act "adjusting the burdens and benefits of economic life"), it is likely that a court would implement rational basis review and uphold the statute.[84] The analysis of economic regulation mandated by the present jurisprudence of substantive due process requires only that Congress act rationally and reasonably, that its decisions need only be within the parameters of the possible approaches that Congress may take. Thus, as indicated by the congressional findings accompanying the minimum essential coverage requirement, given that Congress enacted the requirement in an effort, for example, to increase the number and share of Americans who are insured" and "improve financial security for families," the requirement could be seen as rationally related to these goals, even if other legislative means might be presumed more effective in achieving them.[85] Someone seeking to challenge the minimum essential coverage requirement would likely have to demonstrate to a court that Congress's decision to enact the requirement was arbitrary or irrational. However, it seems unlikely that a reviewing court would see Congress's decision to enact the mandate as irrational, given the deference given to Congress for economic regulation and the importance placed on having health insurance in the U.S. health care system.

Equal Protection

Constitutional challenges that allege discrimination against certain persons are premised either on the equal protection guarantees of the Fourteenth Amendment[86] or the equal protection component of the Fifth Amendment.[87] While the Fourteenth Amendment prohibits discriminatory conduct by the states, the Fifth Amendment forbids such action by the federal government.

It has been said that "[Equal protection] does not reject the government's ability to classify persons or 'draw lines' in the creation and application of laws, but it does guarantee that those classifications will not be based upon impermissible criteria or arbitrarily used to burden a group of individuals."[88] A classification will not offend the Constitution unless it is characterized by invidious discrimination,[89] and the Court has adopted certain levels of review to establish the presence of this discrimination. When a law's classification burdens a fundamental interest (e.g., privacy, marriage, or voting) or there is a suspect classification (e.g., race or country of origin), strict scrutiny is applied. A classification will survive strict scrutiny if the government can show that it is necessary to achieving a compelling state interest.[90] By contrast, when the challenged law does not involve a fundamental right or a suspect classification, a court may undertake rational basis review. This least restrictive form of judicial review allows a classification to survive an equal protection challenge if the classification is rationally related to a legitimate government interest.[91] This level of review is characterized by its deference to legislative judgment. Most economic regulations are subject to rational basis review.[92]

In addition, similar to other economic regulation, classifications made for federal tax purposes are generally constitutionally permissible so long as "they bear a rational relation to a legitimate governmental purpose."[93] Courts typically show great deference to the tax classifications made by legislatures in recognition of "the large area of discretion which is needed by a legislature in formulating sound tax policies."[94] The Supreme Court has noted that, "[i]t has ... been pointed out that in taxation, even more than in other fields, legislatures possess the greatest freedom in classification."[95] Because legislatures have "especially broad latitude" in creating tax classifications,[96] the bar is low for Congress to adequately justify its rationale for making the classifications used.[97] Nevertheless, some tax classifications based on a suspect classification, or that interfere with a fundamental right are subject to higher levels of scrutiny.[98]

Under the minimum essential coverage requirement of PPACA, questions regarding equal protection may arise due to the fact that the requirement to enroll in health coverage and the corresponding tax only apply to certain individuals. For example, as mentioned above, individuals who have coverage through a federal health care program such as Medicare would be deemed to have met the minimum essential coverage requirements. Under PPACA, exemptions from the tax would be made for various individuals, including nonresident aliens, qualified U.S. citizens and residents living abroad, and bona fide residents of the U.S. possessions. Additionally, no penalty would be imposed on individuals who could not afford coverage, taxpayers with income less than 100% of the poverty line, and individuals granted hardship exceptions. While a person subject to the minimum essential coverage requirement could allege discrimination based on the fact that certain other groups would not have to obtain health insurance or pay a tax, the classifications made by these provisions and the corresponding tax seem unlikely to rise to the level of an equal protection violation. Because there does not seem to be a fundamental right that is burdened by the minimum essential coverage requirement,[99] and it appears that no suspect class would be subject to discriminatory treatment, it seems that rational basis scrutiny would be applied by a reviewing court. Also, given that one could envision a legitimate government interest in making the distinction between individuals who, for example, have higher incomes and those who have lower incomes and may have difficulty finding affordable health insurance coverage, an equal protection challenge to the minimum essential coverage requirements or the corresponding taxes would likely be unsuccessful.

Takings Clause

Under the Takings Clause of the Fifth Amendment, no property shall be taken for public use without just compensation.[100] As the Supreme Court has explained, the language of the Takings Clause "requires the payment of compensation whenever the government acquires private property for a public purpose."[101] The clause, extensively explicated by the courts in recent decades, seeks to strike a balance between societal goals and the burdens imposed on property owners to achieve those goals. "Property" under the Takings Clause includes land and personal property, both tangible and intangible. Money is also generally held to be property under the clause.[102]

In a few situations, government actions that appear to be obvious appropriations of property are deemed outside the scope of takings law.[103] While the Supreme Court has found that a taking claim may arise when government appropriates money from a specifically identified fund of money,[104] a statute imposing generalized monetary liability has not been considered by courts to be a taking.[105] Thus, with regard to the minimum essential coverage requirement, it is unlikely that a court would find the amounts required as part of the mandate to be paid for insurance to be a taking. This outcome is further emphasized by the fact that there is a benefit obtained with purchase of the insurance that could offset the economic impact of the regulation.[106] Further, it would be unlikely for a court to find the imposition of an excise tax a taking, as the general rule that money paid in taxes is not deemed to be taken, unless the tax is so arbitrary as to be "confiscatory."[107]

Tenth Amendment

The Tenth Amendment provides that the "powers not delegated to the United States by the Constitution, nor prohibited by it to the States, are reserved to the States respectively, or to the people." While this language would appear to represent one of the most clear examples of a federalist principle in the Constitution, it does not appear likely to have a significant impact in relationship to the instant act. While the Tenth Amendment is often cited by the Supreme Court in Commerce Clause cases as a guiding principle of the concept of limited government, the Tenth Amendment by itself appears to only address the process by which the federal government regulates the states.

In *New York v. United States*,[108] Congress had attempted to regulate in the area of low-level radioactive waste. In a 1985 statute, Congress provided that states must either develop legislation on how to dispose of all low-level radioactive waste generated within the state, or the state would be forced to take title to such waste, which would mean that it became the state's responsibility. The Court found that Congress had attempted to require the states to perform the regulation, and decreed that the failure to do so would require the state to deal with the financial consequences of owning large quantities of radioactive waste. In effect, Congress sought to "commandeer" the legislative process of the states.

In the *New York* case, the Court found that this power was not found in the text or structure of the Constitution, and it was thus a violation of the Tenth Amendment. A later case presented the question of the extent to which Congress could regulate through a state's executive branch officers. This case, *Printz v. United States*,[109] involved the Brady Handgun Act. The Brady Handgun Act required state and local law-enforcement officers to conduct background checks on prospective handgun purchasers within five business days of an attempted purchase. After a historical study of federal commandeering of state officials, the Court concluded that commandeering of state executive branch officials was, like commandeering of the legislature, outside of Congress's power, and consequently a violation of the Tenth Amendment.

There does not appear to be a significant argument that the minimum essential coverage requirement would "commandeer" a state legislature or executive branch officials, as the obligations imposed by the individual mandate would be upon individuals. Consequently, under existing case law, it would not appear that there would be a significant argument that the act would violate the Tenth Amendment.

Religious Exemptions to Minimum Essential Coverage Requirements

Requiring individuals to obtain health insurance may conflict with some individuals' religious beliefs.[110] Accordingly, legislation that would require individuals to obtain health insurance might raise constitutional issues of religious freedom and equal protection.[111] These issues may be addressed with a religious exemption to the minimum essential coverage requirement. Potential religious exemptions must meet the requirements of the First Amendment's religion clauses, which serve as guarantees that individuals will neither be required to act under a prescribed religious belief (the Establishment Clause) nor be prohibited from acting under their chosen religious beliefs (the Free Exercise Clause). Religious exemptions also may raise equal protection issues under the Fifth Amendment. It is important to note that the outcome of the legal analysis under the First Amendment may differ based on the form of the requirement proposed.

Constitutional and Statutory Rules Regarding Religious Exercise

Constitutional and statutory rules regarding free exercise of religion would determine whether a religious exemption would be required for legislation requiring individuals to have health insurance. The First Amendment of the U.S. Constitution provides that "Congress shall make no law respecting an establishment of religion, or prohibiting the free exercise thereof.... "[112] These clauses are known respectively as the Establishment Clause and the Free Exercise Clause. Although the U.S. Supreme Court historically had applied a heightened standard of review to government actions that allegedly interfered with a person's free exercise of religion,[113] the Court reinterpreted that standard in 1990. Since then, the Court has held that the Free Exercise Clause never "relieve[s] an individual of the obligation to comply with a valid and neutral law of general applicability."[114] Under this interpretation, the constitutional baseline of protection was lowered, meaning that laws that do not specifically target religion or do not allow for individualized assessments are not subject to heightened review under the Constitution.

In 1993, Congress enacted the Religious Freedom Restoration Act (RFRA), which statutorily reinstated the heightened standard of review for government actions interfering with a person's free exercise of religion. Although the Court later struck down as unconstitutional portions of RFRA that applied to state and local governments, the heightened standard provided by RFRA still applies to federal government actions.[115] RFRA provides that a statute or regulation of general applicability may lawfully burden a person's exercise of religion only if it (1) furthers a compelling governmental interest, and (2) uses the least restrictive means to further that interest.[116] This two-part standard is sometimes referred to as strict scrutiny analysis. The Supreme Court has held that in order for the government to prohibit exemptions to generally applicable laws, the government must "demonstrate a compelling interest in uniform application of a particular program by offering evidence that granting the requested religious accommodations would seriously compromise its ability to administer the program."[117] Although RFRA currently applies as a general limitation on federal actions, Congress may amend its scope or may exempt future statutes from complying with RFRA.[118] Thus, when considering proposed legislation that may conflict with requirements imposed by RFRA, Congress may avoid the conflict by exempting the legislation from RFRA.

Legal Analysis of Religious Exemptions for the Minimum Essential Coverage Requirement

Analysis of the issues raised by religious exemptions for the minimum essential coverage requirement must address two questions: (1) whether the U.S. Constitution requires a religious exemption to ensure the free exercise rights of individuals who may have religious objections to health insurance; and (2) if a religious exemption is not constitutionally required, but included nonetheless, whether it would be constitutional under the First and Fifth Amendments. The issues addressed in this section stem from religious exemptions offered in other contexts, and some issues that may be raised by future proposals may not be discussed.

Is a Religious Exemption Constitutionally or Statutorily Required for a Minimum Essential Coverage Requirement?

As a neutral law of general applicability that potentially burdens religious exercise, the minimum essential coverage requirement would be subject to analysis under RFRA. Generally, it does not appear that a religious exemption is required for legislation mandating health coverage. The Supreme Court and other lower courts generally have allowed federal mandates that relate to public health, but nonetheless interfere with religious beliefs, to continue without exemptions.[119] Under the strict scrutiny analysis, an exemption would be required only if the government does not have a compelling state interest that is achieved by the least restrictive means possible.

One important goal for enacting the minimum essential coverage requirement appears to be aimed at protecting public health. The government's interest in protecting public health has been held to outweigh individuals' religious interests. According to the Supreme Court, "the right to practice religion freely does not include liberty to expose the community or the child to communicable disease or the latter to ill health or death."[120] The Court delivered this decision before the Court applied a heightened standard of review to religious exercise cases, so it was not required to address whether the government's interest was compelling. Nonetheless, the relative balance struck by the Court between the interests is significant, particularly if a healthcare proposal includes a requirement for children, but not adults. Health care legislation that requires coverage for children may face fewer obstacles in strict scrutiny analysis than legislation requiring coverage for all individuals in part because of the Court's specific recognition that parents' religious liberty does not trump the welfare of children and in part because of the general recognition that children's interests are given heightened protection. In a decision that did apply heightened constitutional review, the Court held that the government's interest in tax programs used to fund health insurance programs for low-income and aging portions of American society outweighs individuals' interests in exercising their religion freely.[121] The Court held that the government had a compelling interest in a uniform tax system that provided revenue for such governmental programs.[122] The Court's treatment of public health as an interest paramount to individual religious practice could be taken to indicate there would be a compelling interest under RFRA.

Although protecting public health through insurance programs appears to be a compelling governmental interest, the nature of the program that promotes public health may be significant to the analysis. For example, medical programs such as laws that require affirmative participation in medical procedures (e.g., vaccinations) differ from financial programs such as laws that require indirect funding of programs aimed at promoting health (e.g., funding for health insurance programs). Because of the varied nature of the burden on religion under these two types of programs, the specific requirements of the legislation impact the determination of constitutionality. In the case of PPACA, the minimum essential coverage requirement is enforced through financial programs and penalties, meaning that the enacted legislation is more likely to avoid constitutional problems than a mandate for affirmative participation in medical programs. Depending on what is deemed to constitute public health, a court may find that requiring individuals to obtain health insurance does not rise to the same level of governmental interest as requirements that directly prevent the spread of disease. On one hand, it may be argued that health insurance coverage promotes productivity in society. Insurance coverage may encourage some individuals to seek medical treatment that they otherwise might forgo if they had to pay the full cost. By seeking treatment, these individuals may have prevented the spread of disease or may have improved their personal health to be more productive members of society. On the other hand, it may be argued that insurance coverage does not promote health because individuals are not guaranteed treatment. The minimum essential coverage requirement does not require individuals to seek or accept treatment, and thus the effectiveness in promoting public health may be questioned.

Even if the government has a compelling interest in requiring individual health insurance, it must use the least restrictive means to achieve that interest in order for the requirement to be upheld as constitutional. That is, the government must make the burden on religious exercise as narrow as possible. This test may be met by providing alternative means of compliance with the legislation, such as the exemption provided in PPACA. Allowing individuals who object to the program on religious grounds and would not receive benefits from the program to opt out of coverage would satisfy both the individual's free exercise of religion and the government's interest in protecting public health at large.

Does the Constitution Allow a Religious Exemption for the Minimum Essential Coverage Requirement?

Even though an exemption may not be required by the Constitution, PPACA's exemption for those with religious objections provides an alternative for certain people based on their religious beliefs that is not available to other people who do not share the same religious beliefs. Thus, some individuals may claim that the religious exemption would violate the Establishment Clause (by providing a benefit to groups based on religion) and the equal protection portion of the Fifth Amendment (by providing for disparate treatment of separate groups).

The Establishment Clause prohibits preferential treatment of one religion over another or preferential treatment of religion generally over nonreligion.[123] Providing an exemption based on religion may be construed as favoring a particular religion or religion generally because only individuals with a religious affiliation would be eligible for the exemption. However, the mere fact that a law addresses religion does not automatically make that law unconstitutional. Traditionally, to be constitutional under Establishment Clause analysis, a government action must meet a three-part test known as the *Lemon* test. To meet the *Lemon* test, a law must (1) have a secular purpose; (2) have a primary effect that neither advances nor inhibits religion; and (3) not lead to excessive entanglement with religion.[124] The Supreme Court has upheld religious exemptions for government programs where the exemptions were enacted to prevent government interference with religious exercise.[125]

Exemptions that are specifically available only to certain religions have been construed in some cases as a violation of the Establishment Clause.[126] The religious conscience exemption in PPACA does not state specific religious groups that would qualify for exemption. Rather PPACA exempts any individual who has been certified to be "a member of a recognized religious sect or division thereof described in section 1402(g)(1) [of the Internal Revenue Code of 1986] and an adherent of established tenets or teaching of such sect or division as described in such section." Section 1402(g)(1) provides an exemption from self-employment income tax if the individual seeking exemption

> is a member of a recognized religious sect or division thereof and is an adherent of established tenets or teachings of such sect or division by reason of which he is conscientiously opposed to acceptance of the benefits of any private or public insurance which makes payments in the event of death, disability, old-age, or retirement or makes payments toward the cost of, or provides services for, medical care.... 127

Thus, the exemption is general, such that any member of any religious organization with the beliefs described in the provision would qualify. This construction of the exemption appears to conform with the constitutional requirements of the First Amendment. The Supreme Court has held that legislation that provides protection or exemption for a specific religious group violates the Establishment Clause of the First Amendment, which forbids preferential treatment based on religion.[128] The Court has held on numerous occasions that the government cannot provide special treatment to one religion over another, or religion generally over non-religion.[129] However, challenges have been made even to generally available religious exemptions under the Establishment Clause because such exemptions would provide preferential treatment to individuals with religious beliefs, but not to individuals who might object on nonreligious philosophical grounds to claim the exemption.[130] Thus, the question of the constitutionality of exemptions based on religion appears not to be settled as of yet.

The concerns of preferential treatment for certain groups of individuals that lead to Establishment Clause questions also raise questions under the equal protection principles of the Fifth Amendment. Equal protection prevents the government from treating some groups of individuals differently from other groups of individuals. If the disparate treatment results from a "suspect classification," equal protection principles may be violated. Typically, courts have recognized groups identified by race, national origin, or alienage as suspect classifications. In the context of religious exemptions, the group being treated differently is a group that might be based on religious affiliation or might be based on nonreligion. Courts often decide cases alleging disparate treatment involving religion under the First Amendment, rather than equal protection. Thus, equal protection jurisprudence does not appear to have addressed religious discrimination to a significant extent. Courts have generally held that laws that treat groups of individuals differently because of some animus would be suspect classifications that would be subject to strict scrutiny. Thus, it appears that the analysis under the equal protection principles likely would not produce a different outcome from the analysis that would be used under the First Amendment.

LEGAL CHALLENGES TO THE MINIMUM ESSENTIAL COVERAGE REQUIREMENT

Several lawsuits have been filed challenging the constitutionality of the minimum essential coverage requirement. While these lawsuits are not identical in their complaints, they typically assert that the federal government does not have the authority to impose on individuals a requirement to purchase health insurance, and therefore seek declarative and injunctive relief. The Administration has filed motions to dismiss in these cases, arguing that the lawsuits are barred because, among other things, the plaintiffs lack standing to challenge the minimum essential coverage requirement, and that the issues asserted are not ripe for adjudication because the requirement does not take effect until 2014, and thus no injury to individuals could occur before then. On the merits, the Administration has contended that the requirement is well within Congress's power under the Commerce Clause, General Welfare Clause, and the Necessary and Proper Clause. Plaintiffs' success in challenging the minimum essential coverage requirement has been mixed.

On the same day that PPACA was signed, attorneys general in 13 states brought an action in the District Court of the Northern District of Florida against the Secretaries of Health and Human Services, Treasury, and Labor, seeking declaratory and injunctive relief from its various requirements.[131] Certain individuals, the National Federation of Independent Business, and several other states later joined this lawsuit, and there are currently 20 state plaintiffs. In *Florida v. HHS*, the plaintiffs claim that the minimum essential coverage requirement exceeds the powers of Congress under the Commerce Clause or the General Welfare Clause and violates the states' rights under the Ninth and Tenth Amendments of the Constitution, as well as individual rights under the Fifth Amendment's Due Process Clause.[132] Alternatively, the plaintiffs allege that the penalty associated with the minimum essential coverage requirement is a direct tax required to be apportioned. On October 14, 2010, the court refused to dismiss the case and held that the Commerce Clause claims against the minimum essential coverage requirement could proceed to the next stage of litigation.[133] At the same time, the court held that the minimum essential coverage requirement was not a tax, and the unapportioned direct tax claims were thus moot.[134] Oral arguments in *Florida v. HHS* were held on December 14, 2010.

Similarly, on the same day that PPACA was signed, the Commonwealth of Virginia challenged the minimum essential coverage requirement on the basis that Congress lacks authority to require individuals to purchase insurance. *Virginia ex rel. Cuccinelli v. Sebelius*[135] was brought in conjunction with the Virginia Health Care Freedom Act, a law stating that Virginia residents cannot be required to obtain or maintain a policy of health insurance coverage, except as required by a court or a state agency.[136] Virginia also alleged that Congress did not have the authority to enact the minimum essential coverage requirement under, among other things, its power to regulate interstate commerce and its taxing power.

On December 13, 2010, the court ruled that the minimum essential coverage requirement is unconstitutional because it exceeds the boundaries of Congress's authority under the Commerce Clause.[137] The court explained that in order for a statute to survive a constitutional challenge under the Commerce Clause, it must, among other things, involve a self-initiated activity. Requiring the advance purchase of insurance based on a future need for health care services, the court found, is not an activity supported by Commerce Clause jurisprudence.[138] The court also held that the General Welfare Clause does not provide authority for Congress to enact the minimum essential coverage requirement, as it most closely resembles a penalty as opposed to a tax. Although it found the minimum essential coverage requirement unconstitutional, the court did not strike down the entire statute. Instead, it severed the minimum essential coverage requirement and "directly-dependent provisions which make reference" to the section from the rest of the Act.[139] In addition, given that the court found no likelihood of irreparable harm pending appellate review, it denied the Commonwealth's request for injunctive relief, thus allowing implementation of the remainder of PPACA to move forward.

In contrast to the Florida and Virginia cases, other plaintiffs have not been as successful in challenging the minimum essential coverage requirement. Some district courts have dismissed plaintiffs' claims for procedural reasons such as lack of standing to bring the action,[140] and two have dismissed challenges on the basis that the requirement is constitutional under the Commerce Clause. In *Thomas More Law Center v. Obama*,[141] the court found that the federal requirement to purchase health insurance, "which addresses economic decisions regarding health care services that everyone eventually, and inevitably, will need, is a reasonable means of effectuating Congress's goal."[142] The court also found that it is essential to the larger regulatory scheme of PPACA. As the court explained, given that PPACA compels insurers to provide policies to any individuals who apply for them, the requirement to purchase health insurance is necessary in order assure that individuals do not wait until they need care to purchase insurance, as this would be detrimental to the insurance market. In *Liberty University v. Geithner*,[143] the U.S. District Court for the Western District of Virginia employed similar reasoning in dismissing a lawsuit brought by a private Christian university and others. Because these courts found the minimum essential coverage requirement constitutional under the Commerce Clause, they did not evaluate whether it would also have been justifiable under the taxing power.[144] Both of these cases have been appealed to the circuit courts.

End Notes

[1] Patient Protection and Affordable Care Act, P.L. 111-148, § 1501(b) (2010), as amended by the Health Care and Education Reconciliation Act of 2010 P.L. 111-152 § 1002 (2010). The requirement to purchase health insurance will be referred to, as in section 1501(b), as the minimum essential coverage requirement.

[2] *See* Congressional Budget Office Memorandum, The Budgetary Treatment of an Individual Mandate to Buy Health Insurance (Aug. 1994) ("A mandate requiring all individuals to purchase health insurance would be an unprecedented form of federal action.").

[3] *See* Mark A. Hall, *The Constitutionality of Mandates to Purchase Health Insurance, Legal Solutions in Health Care Reform*, available at http://www.rwjf.org/files/research/38108. 3693. constitutionality.mandates.pdf. *See also* In Ex Parte Poresky, 290 U.S. 30 (1933) (Court agreed that a district court's dismissal of a complaint alleging that Massachusetts' compulsory automobile liability insurance law violated the 14th Amendment was proper "in view of the decisions of this Court bearing upon the constitutional authority of the State, acting in the interest of public safety, to enact the statute assailed."). It should be noted that while laws related to military service (e.g., the draft) could be considered an example of a federal mandate pertaining to individuals, the authority for these laws likely relies on Congress's authority to raise and support armies. *See generally* Rostker v. Goldberg, 453 U.S. 57, 65 (1981); Selective Draft Law Cases, 245 U.S. 366 (1918).

[4] P.L. 111-148, § 1501(b), as amended by P.L. 111-152, § 1002.

[5] The tax would be one half the applicable dollar amount if the taxpayer was younger than 18 years old.

[6] The filing threshold for individuals is defined in I.R.C. § 6012(a)(1) and is roughly equal to the taxpayer's personal exemption (or exemptions in the case of a joint filer) and standard deduction.

[7] In general, an individual will be deemed not to afford coverage if the required contribution for employer-sponsored coverage or a bronze-level plan on an Exchange exceeds 8% of the individual's household income for the taxable year. *See* 26 U.S.C. § 5000A(e)(1)(A), as created by PPACA. For information on Exchanges as provided for in PPACA, see CRS Report R40942, *Private Health Insurance Provisions in the Patient Protection and Affordable Care Act (PPACA)*, by Hinda Chaikind, Bernadette Fernandez, and Mark Newsom.

[8] *See*, e.g., United States v. Doremus, 249 U.S. 86, 93 (1919) ("If the legislation enacted has some reasonable relation to the exercise of the taxing authority conferred by the Constitution, it cannot be invalidated because of the supposed motives which induced it.").

[9] *See* I.R.C. § 106 (excluding from gross income compensation received by employees in the form of health care benefits).

[10] *But see* Brian D. Galle, Conditional Taxation and the Constitutionality of Health Care Reform (April 3, 2010). Yale Law Journal Online, Forthcoming; FSU College of Law, Public Law Research Paper; GWU Law School Public Law Research Paper. Available at SSRN: http://ssrn.com/abstract=1584044 (arguing "'conditional' taxes—taxes used to achieve some regulatory end—are not limited only to those purposes covered by Congress's other enumerated powers. Instead, Congress may condition exemptions from a tax on any criteria it chooses—other than those expressly prohibited by the Constitution, such as restrictions on free speech—so long as it is willing to pay the political price for carving out that exception.").

[11] Sunshine Anthracite Coal Co. v. Adkins, 310 U.S. 381, 383 (1940) (a tax on coal producers who did not meet certain federal requirements was upheld because the imposition of federal requirements was a valid exercise of Congress' power to regulate interstate commerce).

[12] Child Labor Tax Case, 259 U.S. 20 (1922) (striking tax on the employment of children because regulation of child labor was not within Congress' authority under the Commerce Clause at the time; Congress' authority under the Commerce Clause has since been recognized by the Supreme Court to be much broader).

[13] *Id.* at 38 (emphasis added).

[14] *See* P.L. 111-148, § 1501(a)(2)(A).

[15] *Child Labor Cases*, 259 U.S. at 38 ("To give such magic to the word "tax" would be to break down all constitutional limitation of the powers of Congress and completely wipe out the sovereignty of the States.").

[16] *Id.* at 36-37 ("In the light of these features of the act, a court must be blind not to see that the so-called tax is imposed to stop the employment of children within the age limits prescribed. Its prohibitory and regulatory effect and purpose are palpable. All others can see and understand this. How can we properly shut our minds to it?").

[17] *See* Thomas v. United States, 192 U.S. 363, 370 (1904) ("And these two classes, [direct taxes], and 'duties, imposts and excises," apparently embrace all forms of taxation contemplated by thc Constitution.").

[18] U.S. CONST. Art. 1, § 9, cl. 4 ("No Capitation, or other direct, Tax shall be laid, unless in Proportion to the Census or Enumeration...."); Art. 1, § 2, cl. 3 ("direct Taxes shall be apportioned among the several States....").

[19] U.S. CONST. Art. I, § 8, cl. 1 ("[A]ll duties, Imposts and Excises shall be uniform throughout the United States.").

[20] U.S. CONST. Amend. XVI ("The Congress shall have power to lay and collect taxes on incomes, from whatever source derived, without apportionment among the several States, and without regard to any census or enumeration.").

[21] *See* United States v. Ptasynski, 461 U.S. 74 (1983) (stating the Uniformity Clause bars geographic discrimination).

[22] *See, e.g.,* 2 Farrand's Records 350 ("Mr King asked what was the precise meaning of direct taxation? No one answd."). Primary sources from the time period have supported multiple interpretations, from narrow definitions limiting direct taxes to only those that can realistically be apportioned, perhaps just capitation and real property taxes, to broader interpretations that would, for example, include all taxes other than consumption taxes. *See, e.g.,* Bruce Ackerman, *Taxation and the Constitution,* 99 COLUM. L. REV. 1, 14-19 (1999) (arguing that "direct tax" was primarily a political, and not economic, term intended to be interpreted narrowly); Erik M. Jensen, *The Taxing Power, the Sixteenth Amendment, and the Meaning of "Incomes,"* 33 ARIZ. ST. L.J. 1057 (2001) (arguing that the Framers distinguished the two types on the basis that indirect taxes—which he thinks means taxes on consumption—have inherent protection from government abuse because taxpayers can choose whether to consume if the tax gets too high).

[23] Congress has in the past levied taxes on property. In 1813, Congress levied a direct tax on property totaling three million dollars, which the statute apportioned among the 18 states and then among the counties (parishes) of each state. Act of August 2, 1813, 2 Stat. 53. Thus, for example, $369,018.44 was apportioned to Virginia and $6,354.50 of that amount apportioned to Fairfax County. Provisions for assessing and collecting the tax were contained in the Act of July 22, 1813. 3 Stat. 22 (1813). A direct tax on property totaling $20 million was levied in 1861, apportioned among the states, territories, and the District of Columbia. Act of August 5, 1861, § 8, 12 Stat. 295. We have found no examples of head taxes enacted by Congress.

[24] *See* Hylton v. United States, 3 U.S. 171 (1796). *But, see id. at* 175 (Chase, J., concurring, "I am inclined to think, but of this I do not give a judicial opinion, that the direct taxes contemplated by the Constitution, are only two, to wit, a capitation, or poll tax, simply, *without regard to property, profession, or any other circumstances*; and a tax on land") (emphasis added).

[25] *See* Hylton, 3 U.S. at 175 (upholding unapportioned tax on carriages); Pacific Insurance Co. v. Soule, 74 U.S. 433 (1869) (upholding tax on the business of insurance); Veazie Bank v. Fenno, 75 U.S. 533 (1869) (upholding tax on bank notes); Scholey v. Rew, 90 U.S. 331 (1875) (upholding inheritance tax); Springer v. United States, 102 U.S. 586 (1881) (upholding income tax).

[26] 28 Stat. 509 (1894) (imposing a tax on "the gains, profits, and income received in the preceding calendar year by every citizen of the United States ... whether said gains, profits, or income be derived from any kind of property, rents, interest, dividends, or salaries, or from any profession, trade, employment, or vocation carried on in the United States or elsewhere.... ").

[27] The Court reasoned that income taxes on the gains derived from investments in real or personal property had a substantial impact on the underlying assets and should be treated as direct taxes falling on the property. *See* Pollock, 157 U.S. at 583.

[28] Some commentators would argue the decision has essentially been erased by the Court's subsequent jurisprudence and passage of the Sixteenth Amendment. *See, e.g.,* Calvin H. Johnson, *Fixing the Constitutional Absurdity of the Apportionment of Direct Tax*, 21 CONST. COMMENT. 295, 298-99 (2004) ("Pollock is dead on its holding as to the income tax. Indeed, courts have a duty to distinguish Pollock in every case."). On the other hand, some have argued that "the reports of Pollock's demise are exaggerated" and that "[a]n income tax is nothing like

the classic forms of indirect taxation, and the Supreme Court therefore got the result right in [Pollock]: an income tax is a direct tax as that term was originally understood." Erik M. Jensen, *The Apportionment of "Direct Taxes": Are Consumption Taxes Constitutional?*, 97 COLUM. L. REV. 2334, 2345 (1997); Jensen, *supra* note 23 at 1079.

[29] *See* Nicol v. Ames, 173 U.S. 509 (1899) (tax on certain sales and exchanges of property); Knowlton v. Moore, 178 U.S. 41 (1900) (estate tax); Patton v. Brady, 184 U.S. 609 (1902) (tax on manufactured tobacco); Flint v. Stone Tracy Co., 220 U.S. 107 (1911) (corporate franchise tax); *but see* Eisner v. Macomber, 252 U.S. 189 (1920) (striking an unapportioned tax on a stock dividend that did not change the taxpayer's proportionate ownership of the company, relying on the *Pollock* holding that taxes on rents and income from real and personal property were direct taxes).

[30] *See* Nicol v. Ames, 173 U.S. 509 (1899) (tax on certain sales and exchanges of property); Knowlton v. Moore, 178 U.S. 41 (1900) (estate tax); Patton v. Brady, 184 U.S. 609 (1902) (tax on manufactured tobacco); Flint v. Stone Tracy Co., 220 U.S. 108 (1911) (tax on corporate franchise).

[31] *See also* Galle, *supra* note 11 (arguing the tax could be characterized as imposed on "the use of personal wealth for purposes other than the purchase of health insurance" or "on a particular form of arranging one's economic affairs: the choice to shift the risk of future medical needs from oneself to the social safety net—in effect, a tax on the use of the existing system of free care, medicaid, and debtor-protection and bankruptcy law").

[32] Other provisions include the excise taxes on the failure of tax-exempt private foundations to distribute income (26 U.S.C. § 4942); failures of certain group health plans to provide continuation coverage or to meet certain requirements (26 U.S.C. §§ 4980B, 4980D) and failures of certain investment vehicles to distribute income (26 U.S.C. §§ 4981, 4982).

[33] *See* George Clark, *Baucus "Excise" on Those Who Fail to Buy Insurance Raises Constitutional Issues*, DAILY TAX REPORT, Sept. 29, 2009.

[34] *Id.*

[35] *Id.*

[36] *See, e.g.*, 26 U.S.C. § 163(h) (permitting individuals to deduct qualifying home mortgage interest payments); 26 U.S.C. § 36 (providing a tax credit to qualifying "first-time" homebuyers).

[37] Md. Dec. of R. art. 15.

[38] 31 A. 322 (Md. 1895). Examples of poll taxes recited in the opinion were a specific sum levied on all persons, male or female, free or slave, above the age of 16 for general support of the government and a tax of 40 pounds of tobacco "per poll" to support clergy of the Church of England.

[39] U.S. Const., Art. I, §8, cl. 3. It should be noted that the Commerce Clause is augmented by the Necessary and Proper Clause, which allows Congress "[t]o make all Laws which shall be necessary and proper for carrying into Execution the foregoing Powers ... " U.S. Const., Art. I, §8, cl. 18.

[40] For instance, Chief Justice Marshall wrote in 1824 that "the power over commerce ... is vested in Congress as absolutely as it would be in a single government ..." and that "the influence which their constituents possess at elections, are ... the sole restraints" on this power. Gibbons v. Odgen, 22 U.S. (9 Wheat.) 1, 197-98 (1824).

[41] See CRS Report RL32844, *The Power to Regulate Commerce: Limits on Congressional Power*, by Kenneth R. Thomas and Todd B. Tatelman.

[42] 322 U.S. 533 (1944). In response to the Court's ruling in *South-Eastern Underwriters,* Congress explicitly recognized the role of the states in the regulation of insurance with the passage of the McCarran-Ferguson Act of 1945. The intent of the McCarran-Ferguson Act was to grant states

the explicit authority to regulate insurance in light of the *South-Eastern Underwriters* decision. Section 2(a) of the Act states: The business of insurance, and every person engaged therein, shall be subject to the laws of the several States which relate to the regulation or taxation of such business. 15 U.S.C. § 1012(a). However, under the Act, Congress also reserved to itself the right to enact federal statutes that "specifically" relate to "the business of insurance." 15 U.S.C. § 1012(b).

[43] *See* United States v. Lopez, 514 U.S. 549, 558-59 (1995) (internal citations omitted).

[44] 529 U.S. 598 (2000).

[45] 545 U.S. 1 (2005).

[46] 317 U.S. 111 (1942).

[47] *See Lopez*, 514 U.S. at 557; *Morrison*, 529 U.S. at 608.

[48] In 1941, Mr. Filburn harvested an excess amount of 239 bushels for which he was fined pursuant to amendments to the Agricultural Adjustment Act of 1938. 317 U.S. at 114.

[49] *Id.* at 125.

[50] *Id.*

[51] *Lopez*, 514 U.S. at 564.

[52] *Morrison*, 529 U.S at 613.

[53] The Court pointed to various legislative findings including findings that gender-motivated violence affected interstate commerce by deterring potential victims from traveling interstate, from engaging in interstate business, by diminishing national productivity, and increasing medical and other costs. *Id.* at 615 (quoting H.Rept. 103-711, at 385).

[54] *Id.*

[55] *Id.* It should be noted that after the decision in *Lopez* and *Morrison*, the question arose as to whether these cases were an indicator of future restrictions on Congress's power to regulate interstate commerce. However, it is arguable that the Court intended *Lopez* and *Morrison* to have a limited effect, as the Court specifically reaffirmed much of its previous Commerce Clause case law, including *Wickard.*

[56] *Raich*, 545 U.S. at 18.

[57] *Id.* at 25. The Court explained that "the CSA regulates the production, distribution, and consumption of commodities for which there is an established, and lucrative, interstate market. Prohibiting the intrastate possession or manufacture of an article of commerce is a rational ... means of regulating commerce in that product." Id. at 26.

[58] *Id.* at 26-27. *See also Lopez*, 514 U.S., at 561.

[59] As discussed above, after *Lopez* and *Morrison*, whether a regulation has a substantial effect on interstate commerce requires reviewing courts to consider the following four factors: (1) whether the regulated activity is commercial or economic in nature; (2) whether an express jurisdictional element is provided in the statute to limit its reach; (3) whether Congress made express findings about the effects of the activity on interstate commerce; and (4) whether the link between the activity and the effect on interstate commerce is attenuated. United States v. Stewart, 348 F.3d 1132, 1136-37 (9th Cir. 2003) (citing *Morrison*, 529 U.S. at 610-12).

[60] Centers for Medicare and Medicaid Services, National Health Expenditure Data Fact Sheet, *available at* http://www.cms.gov/NationalHealthExpendData/25_NHE_Fact_Sheet.asp.

[61] *See*, e.g., Perez v. U.S., 402 U.S. 146 (1971) (conviction for loan sharking affirmed because Consumer Credit Protection Act held to be a valid exercise of the Commerce Clause); United States v. Ogba, 526 F.3d 214 (5th Cir. 2008) (health care fraud statute acceptable under Commerce Clause); United States v. Bishop, 66 F.3d 569(3rd Cir. 1995), *cert. denied* 516 U.S. 1032 (1995) (Congress had not exceeded its power under the Commerce Clause in enacting a carjacking statute).

[62] *Id. But see* the dissent in Bishop, 66 F.3d at 592 (Becker, J., dissenting) (arguing that Congress's Commerce Clause power under the substantially affects category is limited to regulation of "a voluntary economic exchange.").

[63] 18 U.S.C. § 228.

[64] P.L. 111-148, § 1501(a)(2).

[65] *See generally* David B. Rivkin Jr. and Lee A. Casey, Mandatory Insurance Is Unconstitutional, Wall Street Journal, Sept. 18, 2009 (arguing that "Congress could evade all constitutional limits by "taxing" anyone who doesn't follow an order of any kind—whether to obtain health-care insurance, or to join a health club, or exercise regularly, or even eat your vegetables.")

[66] P.L. 111-148, §1501(a)(2).

[67] Further, if a court finds the minimum essential coverage requirement to be, similar to the provisions in Wickard and Raich, an essential component of a larger economic regulatory scheme, then the need for a jurisdictional element may be alleviated. *See* discussion of Raich *infra*.

[68] It may be noted that Congress replaced the provision struck down in *Lopez* with an amended version that makes it unlawful for an individual "knowingly to possess a firearm *that has moved in or that otherwise affects interstate or foreign commerce* at a place that the individual knows, or has reasonable cause to believe, is a school zone." See 18 U.S.C. § 922(q)(2)(A) (emphasis added). This amendment demonstrates that the required nexus to interstate commerce can, at least in some cases, may be fixed.

[69] *See, e.g.*, Health Care Affordability and the Uninsured, Testimony of Diane Rowland to the House of Representatives, Committee on Ways and Means, Health Subcommittee, available at http://www.kff.org/uninsured

[70] P.L. 111-148, § 1501(a)(2).

[71] The Court has also suggested that challenges to non-commercial aspects of a larger economic regulatory scheme may be evaluated under the Necessary and Proper Clause. *Raich*, 545 U.S at 36 (Scalia, J., concurring) ("Congress' authority to enact laws necessary and proper for the regulation of interstate commerce is not limited to laws directed against economic activities that have a substantial effect on interstate commerce."). Using this rationale, it could be argued that a requirement that individuals obtain health insurance is necessary for the proper functioning of the broader health care regulation established under PPACA, so that such a mandate would pass Constitutional muster. *Id.* at 22. The kinds of factors likely to be considered are (1) the historic breadth of the Necessary and Proper Clause; (2) the history of federal involvement in this area; (3) the reason for the statute's enactment; (4) the statute's accommodation of state interests; and (5) whether the scope of the statute is too attenuated from Article I powers. United States v. Comstock, No. 08–1224 slip. op. (May 17, 2010).

[72] P.L. 111-148, § 1501(a)(2).

[73] See e.g., Peter Urbanowicz and Dennis G. Smith, Constitutional Implications of an "Individual Mandate" in Health Care Reform, The Federalist Society for Law and Public Policy Studies, available at http://www.fed-soc.org/doclib/ 20090710_Individual_ Mandates.pdf. But see generally Simon Lazarus, Mandatory Health Insurance, Is It Constitutional? American Constitutional Society Issue for Law and Policy Issue Brief, available at http://www.acslaw.org/pdf/Lazarus%20Issue%20Brief%20Final.pdf.

[74] U.S. Const. Amend. V. See also U.S. Const. Amend. XIV, §1, which contains a similar clause that applies to states.

[75] Roe v. Wade, 410 U.S. 113, 155 (1973). *See also* Carey v. Population Services Int'l, 431 U.S. 678, 686 (1977). Fundamental rights found by the Court include the right to use contraception, marry, procreate, have family relationships, and control the education of one's children.

[76] Among its substantive due process cases, the Court has held that welfare benefits, housing, federal employment, a funded education, pregnancy-related medical care, and medically necessary abortions are not fundamental rights, and it evaluated the statutes under a rational basis review. William P. Gunnar, *Article: The Fundamental Law That Shapes the United States Health Care System: Is Universal Health Care Realistic Within the Established Paradigm*? 15 Ann. Health L. 151 (2006).

[77] While the U.S. Constitution does not explicitly set forth a right to health care, the Supreme Court's decisions in the areas of the right to privacy and bodily integrity suggest the Constitution implicitly provides an individual the right to access or deny health care services at one's own expense from willing medical providers. *See* Roe v. Wade, 410 U.S. 113 (1973) (constitutionally protected right to choose whether or not to terminate a pregnancy) *and* Cruzan v. Missouri Department of Health, 497 U.S. 261 (1990) (constitutional right to refuse medical treatment that sustains life), both of which involve a right to bodily integrity that may be extended to a person seeking health care services at his or her own expense. For a general discussion of constitutional rights related to health care, *see* CRS Report R40846, *Health Care: Constitutional Rights and Legislative Powers*, by Kathleen S. Swendiman.

[78] In challenging the minimum essential coverage requirement on due process grounds, it is possible that one could allege a fundamental right to not purchase health insurance. However, this is not a fundamental right that has been recognized by the Supreme Court. *But see* Roy G. Spece, Jr., *Article: A Fundamental Constitutional Right of the Monied to "Buy Out Of" Universal Health Care Program Restrictions Versus the Moral Claim of Everyone Else to Decent Health Care: An Unremitting Paradox of Health Care Reform?* 3 J. Health & Biomed. L. 1 (2007) (alleging that "many would argue that persons surely have a fundamental right to purchase standard [health] care and insurance necessary to obtain that care").

[79] Griswold v. Connecticut, 381 U.S. 479 (1965) (quoting Boyd v. United States, 116 U.S. 616, 630 (1886)).

[80] Arguably, this approach to economic legislation began with *Nebbia v. New York*, 291 U.S. 502 (1934), in which the Court upheld a state statute establishing a commission to fix milk prices as a reasonable health and welfare measure. The Court asked only that state regulation not be unreasonable or arbitrary and that the regulation have a real relation to the object of the legislation. A divided Court in *West Coast Hotel Co. v. Parrish*, 300 U.S. 379 (1937), upheld a state minimum-wage law. "The Constitution does not speak of freedom of contract. It speaks of liberty and prohibits the deprivation of liberty without due process of law.... [R]egulation which is reasonable in relation to its subject and adopted in the interests of the community is due process." *Id.* at 391. For additional background on the history and jurisprudence of economic substantive due process, see Congressional Research Service, CONSTITUTION OF THE UNITED STATES OF AMERICA, ANALYSIS AND INTERPRETATION, p. 1682 et seq.

[81] Usery v. Turner Elkhorn Mining Co., 428 U.S. 1, 15 (1976). See also Concrete Pipe & Products of California, Inc. v. Construction Laborers Pension Fund, 508 U.S. 602, 637-39 (1993).

[82] PBGC v. R. A. Gray & Co., 467 U.S. 717, 729 (1984).

[83] Duke Power Co. v. Carolina Environmental Study Group, 438 U.S. 59, 83-4 (1978).

[84] It should be noted that even if a court were not to consider a requirement to purchase health insurance as "economic regulation," it is still likely that a court would evaluate a requirement to purchase health insurance under a rational basis review, given the absence of a fundamental right.

[85] §1501(a) of P.L. 111-148.

[86] U.S. Const. Amend. XIV, § 1. The Fourteenth Amendment provides, in relevant part, No State shall make or enforce any law which shall abridge the privileges or immunities of citizens of the

United States; nor shall any State deprive any person of life, liberty, or property, without due process of law; nor deny to any person within its jurisdiction the equal protection of the laws.

[87] The Equal Protection Clause of the Fourteenth Amendment, which by its terms applies only to the states, has been held applicable to the federal government as well through the Due Process Clause of the Fifth Amendment. A 1995 Supreme Court decision notes that the Court has for decades "treat[ed] the equal protection obligations imposed by the Fifth and Fourteenth Amendments as indistinguishable." Adarand Constructors, Inc. v. Pena, 515 U.S. 200, 217 (1995). See also Buckley v. Valeo, 424 U.S. 1, 93 (1976) ("Equal protection analysis in the Fifth Amendment area," the Court has said, "is the same as that under the Fourteenth Amendment.").

[88] Ronald D. Rotunda and John E. Nowak, Treatise on Constitutional Law: Substance and Procedure § 18.2 (3d ed. 1999).

[89] *See* Ferguson v. Skrupa, 372 U.S. 726, 732 (1963).

[90] *See* San Antonio Independent School District v. Rodriquez, 411 U.S. 1 (1973).

[91] It should be noted that the Court has also recognized an intermediate level of scrutiny. See Craig v. Boren, 429 U.S. 190, 197 (1976). A classification will survive intermediate scrutiny if it is substantially related to achieving an important government objective. Sex classifications are subject to intermediate scrutiny.

[92] The Supreme Court has opined that "In areas of social and economic policy, a statutory classification that neither proceeds along suspect lines nor infringes fundamental constitutional rights must be upheld against equal protection challenge if there is any reasonably conceivable state of facts that could provide a rational basis for the classification.... Where there are 'plausible reasons' for Congress' action, 'our inquiry is at an end.'" FCC v. Beach Communications, 508 U.S. 307, 313-314 (1993) (quoting United States Railroad Retirement Bd. v. Fritz, 449U.S. 166, 179 (1980)).

[93] Regan v. Taxation with Representation of Washington, 461 U.S. 540, 547 (1983).

[94] Taxation with Representation, 461 U.S. at 547 (*quoting* Madden v. Kentucky, 309 U.S. 83, 88 (1940)).

[95] *Id.* (*quoting* Madden, 309 U.S. at 88).

[96] *Id.*

[97] *See id.* at 547-48 ("'[T]he presumption of constitutionality can be overcome only by the most explicit demonstration that a classification is a hostile and oppressive discrimination against particular persons and classes. The burden is on the one attacking the legislative arrangement to negative every conceivable basis which might support it.' Madden v. Kentucky, 309 U.S. 83, 87-88 (1940)").

[98] *See Taxation with Representation of Washington*, 461 U.S. at 547.

[99] As previously discussed, neither the Constitution nor the Supreme Court's jurisprudence suggests a fundamental right to health care. *See* discussion of Substantive Due Process *supra*.

[100] For a general discussion of takings law, *see* CRS Report RS20741, *The Constitutional Law of Property Rights "Takings": An Introduction*, by Robert Meltz, *The Constitutional Law of Property Rights 'Takings': An Introduction*, by Robert Meltz.

[101] Brown v. Legal Found., 538 U.S. 216, 232 (2003).

[102] Phillips v. Wash. Legal Found., 524 U.S. 156, 160 (1998); Webb's Fabulous Pharms., Inc. v. Beckwith, 449 U.S. 155, 164-65 (1980). *See generally* Eastern Enterprises v. Apfel, 524 U.S. 498, 540, 554 (1998) (in a plurality opinion, five justices opine that regulatory actions requiring the payment of money are not takings).

[103] Robert Meltz, *Takings Law Today: A Primer for the Perplexed*, 34 ECOLOGY L.Q. 307, 327 (2007).

104 Brown v. Legal Found., 538 U.S. 216, 232 (2003); Webb's Fabulous Pharms., Inc. v. Beckwith, 449 U.S. 155 (1980).

105 *See*, e.g., Commonwealth Edison Co. v. United States, 271 F.3d 1327, 1338-40 (Fed. Cir. 2001) (en banc); Swisher International, Inc. v. Shafer, 550 F.3d 1046 (11th Cir. 2008). *See generally* Eastern Enterprises v. Apfel, 524 U.S. 498, 540, 554 (1998) (in a plurality opinion, five justices opined that regulatory actions requiring the payment of money were not takings).

106 *See* Penn Central Transp. Co. v. New York City, 438 U.S. 104, 137 (1978), where the Supreme Court made clear that certain land development rights conferred on the landowner who claimed to be subject to a taking "mitigate whatever financial burdens the law has imposed ... and ... are to be taken into account in considering the impact of regulation."

107 *See, e.g.*, County of Mobile v. Kimball, 102 U.S. 691, 703 (1880); Branch v. United States, 69 F.3d 1571, 1576-77 (Fed. Cir. 1995) (collecting cases).

108 505 U.S. 144 (1992).

109 521 U.S. 898 (1997).

110 Some religions teach that the religious community must be responsible for social services that otherwise might be included in health insurance coverage. The Amish, for example, believe that the community has an obligation to provide the assistance that would be provided by Medicare programs to community members in need of such assistance, and have challenged laws requiring their participation in such programs as unconstitutional. *See* United States v. Lee, 455 U.S. 252 (1982). Other religions teach that spiritual treatment through prayer, rather than medical treatment, is the appropriate method to treat ailments. *See* Christian Science, 1 Encyclopedia of Politics and Religion 141 (Robert Wuthnow, ed., 2nd ed.) (2006).

111 For background and legal analysis of religious exemptions in mandatory healthcare programs generally, *see* CRS Report RL34708, *Religious Exemptions for Mandatory Health Care Programs: A Legal Analysis*, by Cynthia Brougher.

112 U.S. Const. Amend. I. For a discussion of constitutional and statutory standards of review used in relation to the First Amendment, *see* CRS Report RS22833, *The Law of Church and State: General Principles and Current Interpretations*, by Cynthia Brougher.

113 *See* Wisconsin v. Yoder, 406 U.S. 205 (1972); Sherbert v. Verner, 374 U.S. 398 (1963).

114 Employment Div., Oregon Dep't of Human Resources v. Smith, 494 U.S. 872, 879 (1990).

115 *See* City of Boerne, Texas v. Flores, 521 U.S. 407 (1997).

116 42 U.S.C. § 2000bb-1(b). In some instances, RFRA may be preempted by another federal law. *See* S.Rept. 103-111, at 12-13 (1993).

117 Gonzales v. O Centro Espirita Beneficente Unaio Do Vegetal, 546 U.S. 418, 435-437 (2006).

118 Under the longstanding legal principle of entrenchment, a legislative enactment cannot bind a future Congress. That is, Congress cannot entrench a legislative action by providing that it may not be repealed or altered. *See* Fletcher v. Peck, 10 U.S. 87, 135 (1810) (Chief Justice Marshall).

119 *See, e.g.*, Prince v. Massachusetts, 321 U.S. 158 (1944); Cude v. State, 237 Ark. 927 (1964).

120 Prince, 321 U.S. at 166-67.

121 *Lee*, 455 U.S. at 260-61.

122 *Id.*

123 Epperson v. Arkansas, 393 U.S. 97, 103-04 (1968).

124 Lemon v. Kurtzman, 403 U.S. 602, 612-13 (1971). While the first two prongs of the test are self-explanatory, the third prong prohibits "an intimate and continuing relationship" between government and religion as the result of the law. Id. at 621-22. The continuing viability of *Lemon* has been unclear as the Court has raised questions regarding its adequacy in analyzing these issues. *See, e.g.*, County of Allegheny v. American Civil Liberties Union, 492 U.S. 573 (1989).

[125] In *Locke v. Davey*, the Court recognized that some government actions that allow free exercise consequently raise questions of establishment, noting that there was room for "play in the joints" in this intersection of the religion clauses. 540 U.S. 712 (2004).

[126] *See* Sherr v. Northport-East Northport Union Free School District, 672 F. Supp. 81, 89-90 (E.D.N.Y. 1987).

[127] 26 U.S.C. § 1402(g)(1).

[128] U.S. CONST. amend I. *See* Board of Education of Kiryas Joel v. Grumet, 512 U.S. 687 (1994) (invalidating the creation of a school district for one particular religious group). The Court has looked at whether the religious group alleged to be favored by the act in violation of the Establishment Clause is one of many religious groups eligible for similar treatment or if the special treatment is made through a series of benefits offered separately to multiple groups. *Id.* at 703-704.

[129] *See* Wallace v. Jaffree, 472 U.S. 38, 52-54 (1985); Epperson v. Arkansas, 393 U.S. 97, 104 (1968); School Dist. of Abington Township v. Schempp, 374 U.S. 203, 216-217 (1963).

[130] *See* McCarthy v. Boozman, 212 F.Supp. 2d 945 (W.D. Ark. 2002).

[131] Florida v. Department of Health and Human Services, Case No.: 3:10-cv-91-RV/EMT (N.D. Fla., amended complaint filed May 14, 2010), available at http://healthreformgps.org/wp-content/uploads/Fla-v.-Sebelius.pdf.

[132] The plaintiffs in the Florida lawsuit also allege that the financial burdens imposed on the states by the PPACA's expansion of Medicaid "commandeers" states to devote their financial resources to achieve federal aims, thereby violating the Tenth Amendment to the Constitution. For additional discussion of this issue, *see* CRS Report R40846, *Health Care: Constitutional Rights and Legislative Powers*, by Kathleen S. Swendiman.

[133] Florida v. HHS, No. 3:10-cv-91-RV/EMT, slip op. at 65. The court did permit the state plaintiffs' claims with respect to the Medicaid provisions in PPACA to proceed. These claims are unrelated to the constitutional issues surrounding the individual mandate. *See* CRS Report R40846, *Health Care: Constitutional Rights and Legislative Powers*, by Kathleen S. Swendiman.

[134] Florida v. HHS, No. 3:10-cv-91-RV/EMT, slip op. at 57-58.

[135] Virginia ex rel. Cuccinelli v. Sebelius, No. 3:10cv188-HEH (E.D. Va., filed Dec. 13, 2010).

[136] *See* Va. Code Ann. § 38.2-3430.1:1 (2010), available at http://leg1.state 101+ful+HB10ER2+pdf.

[137] The court mentioned in a footnote that it did not need to address the argument advanced by the Commonwealth that the minimum essential coverage requirement conflicts with the application of the Virginia Health Care Freedom Act. *See* Virginia ex rel. Cuccinelli v. Sebelius, No. 3:10cv188-HEH, slip op. at 9, fn. 4.

[138] *Id.* at 23.

[139] *Id.* at 40. When one section of a law is held unconstitutional, courts are faced with determining whether the remainder of the statute remains valid, or whether the whole statute or act is nullified. As noted by the Supreme Court, "Unless it is evident that the Legislature would not have enacted those provisions which are within its power, independently of that which is not, the invalid part may be dropped if what is left is fully operative as a law." Alaska Airlines, Inc. v. Brock, 480 U.S. 678, 684 (1987) (quoting Buckley v. Valeo, 424 U.S. 1, 108 (1976)). For a discussion of the issue of severability, see CRS Report 97-589, *Statutory Interpretation: General Principles and Recent Trends*, by Larry M. Eig.

[140] *See, e.g.*, New Jersey Physicians, Inc. v. Obama, No. 10-1489 (NJ, filed Dec. 8, 2010); Baldwin v. Sebelius, No. 10- 1033, (S.D. Cal., filed 8/27/10).

[141] Thomas More Law Ctr. v. Obama, 2010 U.S. Dist. LEXIS 107416 (Oct. 7, 2010).

[142] *Id.* at 29.

[143] Liberty Univ., Inc. v. Geithner, 2010 U.S. Dist. LEXIS 125922 (Nov. 30, 2010)

[144] It should be noted, however, that courts finding the minimum essential coverage requirement to be constitutional on Commerce Clause grounds have expressed some doubts as to whether the requirement could be valid under Congress's taxing power. As stated in Liberty University, "[a]lthough the penalties collected under [PPACA] are expected to raise revenue, their main purpose is to enforce the requirement that individuals and employers purchase or provide health insurance. Therefore, the penalty provisions, as 'mere incidents of the regulation of commerce,' ... are not considered taxes for the purpose of the present claim." Liberty Univ., Inc. v. Geithner, 2010 U.S. Dist. LEXIS 125922 at 93. *See also* Thomas More Law Ctr., 2010 U.S. Dist. LEXIS 107416, at 29-31.

In: Mandated Health Care: Constitutional Analysis ISBN: 978-1-61324-162-2
Editor: Jonathan P. Reilly © 2011 Nova Science Publishers, Inc.

Chapter 3

ACTION SEEKING DECLARATORY AND INJUNCTIVE RELIEF FROM THE "PATIENT PROTECTION AND AFFORDABLE CARE ACT"

IN THE UNITED STATES DISTRICT COURT NORTHERN DISTRICT OF FLORIDA Pensacola Division

Case No.: 3:10-cv-91-RV/EMT

**STATE OF FLORIDA, by and through
PAM BONDI, ATTORNEY GENERAL
OF THE STATE OF FLORIDA;**

**STATE OF SOUTH CAROLINA,
by and through ALAN WILSON,
ATTORNEY GENERAL
OF THE STATE OF SOUTH CAROLINA;**

**STATE OF NEBRASKA,
by and through JON BRUNING, A
TTORNEY GENERAL OF THE STATE OF NEBRASKA;**

**STATE OF TEXAS, by and through
GREG ABBOTT, ATTORNEY GENERAL
OF THE STATE OF TEXAS;**

STATE OF UTAH, by and through
MARK L. SHURTLEFF,
ATTORNEY GENERAL OF THE STATE OF UTAH;

STATE OF LOUISIANA, by and through
JAMES D. "BUDDY" CALDWELL,
ATTORNEY GENERAL OF THE STATE OF LOUISIANA;

STATE OF ALABAMA, by and through
LUTHER STRANGE,
ATTORNEY GENERAL OF THE STATE OF ALABAMA;

BILL SCHUETTE, ATTORNEY GENERAL
OF THE STATE OF MICHIGAN,
ON BEHALF OF THE PEOPLE OF MICHIGAN;

STATE OF COLORADO,
by and through
JOHN W. SUTHERS,
ATTORNEY GENERAL
OF THE STATE OF COLORADO;

COMMONWEALTH OF PENNSYLVANIA,
by and through THOMAS W. CORBETT, Jr.,

GOVERNOR OR THE COMMONWEALTH
OF PENNSYLVANIA, and WILLIAM H. RYAN, Jr.,
ACTING ATTORNEY GENERAL
OF THE COMMONWEALTH OF PENNSYLVANIA;

STATE OF WASHINGTON,
by and through ROBERT M. McKENNA, A
TTORNEY GENERAL OF THE STATE OF WASHINGTON;

STATE OF IDAHO, by and through
LAWRENCE G. WASDEN,
ATTORNEY GENERAL
OF THE STATE OF IDAHO;

**STATE OF SOUTH DAKOTA,
by and through
MARTY J. JACKLEY,
ATTORNEY GENERAL OF THE STATE OF SOUTH DAKOTA;**

**STATE OF INDIANA, by and through
GREGORY F. ZOELLER,
ATTORNEY GENERAL
OF THE STATE OF INDIANA;**

**STATE OF NORTH DAKOTA,
by and through
WAYNE STENEHJEM,
ATTORNEY GENERAL
OF THE STATE OF NORTH DAKOTA;**

**STATE OF MISSISSIPPI,
by and through HALEY BARBOUR,
GOVERNOR OF THE STATE OF MISSISSIPPI;**

**STATE OF ARIZONA,
by and through
JANICE K. BREWER,
GOVERNOR OF THE STATE OF ARIZONA,
and THOMAS C. HORNE,
ATTORNEY GENERAL OF THE STATE OF ARIZONA;**

**STATE OF NEVADA,
by and through JIM GIBBONS,
GOVERNOR OF THE STATE OF NEVADA;**

**STATE OF GEORGIA,
by and through SAMUEL S. OLENS,
ATTORNEY GENERAL OF THE STATE OF GEORGIA;**

**STATE OF ALASKA, by and through
DANIEL S. SULLIVAN,
ATTORNEY GENERAL OF THE STATE OF ALASKA;**

STATE OF OHIO, by and through MICHAEL DeWINE, ATTORNEY GENERAL OF THE STATE OF OHIO;

STATE OF KANSAS, by and through DEREK SCHMIDT, ATTORNEY GENERAL OF THE STATE OF KANSAS;

STATE OF WYOMING, by and through MATTHEW H. MEAD, GOVERNOR OF THE STATE OF WYOMING;

STATE OF WISCONSIN, by and through J.B. VAN HOLLEN, ATTORNEY GENERAL OF THE STATE OF WISCONSIN;

STATE OF MAINE, by and through WILLIAM J. SCHNEIDER, ATTORNEY GENERAL OF THE STATE OF MAINE;

TERRY E. BRANSTAD, GOVERNOR OF THE STATE OF IOWA, ON BEHALF OF THE PEOPLE OF IOWA;

NATIONAL FEDERATION OF INDEPENDENT BUSINESS, a California nonprofit mutual benefit corporation;

MARY BROWN, an individual; and KAJ AHLBURG, an individual; Plaintiffs,
v.
UNITED STATES DEPARTMENT OF HEALTH AND HUMAN SERVICES; KATHLEEN SEBELIUS, in her official capacity as the Secretary of the United States Department of Health and Human Services; UNITED STATES DEPARTMENT OF THE TREASURY; TIMOTHY F. GEITHNER, in his official capacity as the Secretary of the United States Department of the Treasury; UNITED STATES DEPARTMENT OF LABOR; and HILDA

L. SOLIS, in her official capacity as Secretary of the United States Department of Labor, Defendants.

SECOND AMENDED COMPLAINT

Pursuant to Rule 15(a), Federal Rules of Civil Procedure, Plaintiffs file this Second Amended Complaint against Defendants and state:

Nature of the Action

1) This is an action seeking declaratory and injunctive relief from the "Patient Protection and Affordable Care Act," P.L. 111-148, as amended by the "Health Care and Education Reconciliation Act of 2010," P.L. 111-152 (collectively the Act). The Act's mandate that all citizens and legal residents of the United States maintain qualifying healthcare coverage or pay a penalty (individual mandate) is an unprecedented encroachment on the sovereignty of the Plaintiff States and on the rights of their citizens, including members of Plaintiff National Federation of Independent Business (NFIB) and individual Plaintiffs Mary Brown and Kaj Ahlburg. By imposing such a mandate, the Act: exceeds the powers of the United States under Article I of the Constitution, particularly the Commerce Clause; violates the Ninth and Tenth Amendments and the Constitution's principles of federalism and dual sovereignty; and violates the Fifth Amendment's Due Process Clause. In the alternative, if the penalty required under the Act is a tax, it constitutes an unlawful capitation or direct tax in violation of Article I, sections 2 and 9 of the Constitution.
2) The Act further violates the Constitution by forcing the Plaintiff States to operate a wholly refashioned Medicaid program. The Act converts Medicaid from a federal-State partnership to provide a safety net for the needy into a federally-imposed universal healthcare regime, in which the discretion of the Plaintiff States has been removed and new requirements and expenses forced upon them in derogation of their sovereignty. In so doing, the Act violates the Ninth and Tenth Amendments and the Constitution's principles of federalism.
3) Plaintiffs seek declaratory and injunctive relief against the Act's operation in order to avoid an unprecedented and unconstitutional

intrusion by the federal government into the private affairs of every American and to preserve Plaintiff States' respective sovereignty, as guaranteed by the Constitution.

Jurisdiction and Venue

4) The Court has subject-matter jurisdiction pursuant to 28 U.S.C. § 1331 because this action arises under the Constitution and laws of the United States and further has jurisdiction to render declaratory relief under 28 U.S.C. § 2201.
5) Venue is proper in this district pursuant to 28 U.S.C. § 1391(e)(3) because no real property is involved, the district is situated in Florida, and the defendants are agencies of the United States or officers thereof acting in their official capacity.

Parties

6) The State of Florida, by and through Pam Bondi, Attorney General of Florida, is a sovereign State in the United States of America.
7) The State of South Carolina, by and through Alan Wilson, Attorney General of South Carolina, is a sovereign State in the United States of America.
8) The State of Nebraska, by and through Jon Bruning, Attorney General of Nebraska, is a sovereign State in the United States of America.
9) The State of Texas, by and through Greg Abbott, Attorney General of Texas, is a sovereign State in the United States of America.
10) The State of Utah, by and through Mark L. Shurtleff, Attorney General of Utah, is a sovereign State in the United States of America.
11) The State of Alabama, by and through Luther Strange, Attorney General of Alabama, is a sovereign State in the United States of America.
12) The State of Louisiana, by and through James D. "Buddy" Caldwell, Attorney General of Louisiana, is a sovereign State in the United States of America.
13) Bill Schuette, Attorney General of Michigan, is bringing this action on behalf of the People of Michigan under Mich. Comp. Law § 14.28, which provides that the Michigan Attorney General may "appear for the people of [Michigan] in any other court or tribunal, in any cause or matter, civil

or criminal, in which the people of [Michigan] may be a party or interested." Under Michigan's constitution, the people are sovereign. Mich. Const. art. I, § 1 ("All political power is inherent in the people. Government is instituted for their equal benefit, security, and protection.").

14) The State of Colorado, by and through John W. Suthers, Attorney General of Colorado, is a sovereign State in the United States of America.

15) The Commonwealth of Pennsylvania, by and through Thomas W. Corbett, Jr., Governor of Pennsylvania, and William H. Ryan, Jr., Acting Attorney General of Pennsylvania, is a sovereign State in the United States of America.

16) The State of Washington, by and through Robert A. McKenna, Attorney General of Washington, is a sovereign State in the United States of America.

17) The State of Idaho, by and through Lawrence G. Wasden, Attorney General of Idaho, is a sovereign State in the United States of America.

18) The State of South Dakota, by and through Marty J. Jackley, Attorney General of South Dakota, is a sovereign State in the United States of America.

19) The State of Indiana, by and through Gregory F. Zoeller, Attorney General of Indiana, is a sovereign State in the United States of America.

20) The State of North Dakota, by and through Wayne Stenehjem, Attorney General of North Dakota, is a sovereign State in the United States of America.

21) The State of Mississippi, by and through Haley Barbour, Governor of Mississippi, is a sovereign State in the United States of America.

22) The State of Arizona, by and through Janice K. Brewer, Governor of Arizona, and Thomas C. Horne, Attorney General of the State of Arizona, is a sovereign State in the United States of America.

23) The State of Nevada, by and through Jim Gibbons, Governor of Nevada, is a sovereign State in the United States of America.

24) The State of Georgia, by and through Samuel S. Olens, Attorney General of Georgia, is a sovereign State in the United States of America.

25) The State of Alaska, by and through Daniel S. Sullivan, Attorney General of Alaska, is a sovereign State in the United States of America.

25A.The State of Ohio, by and through Michael DeWine, Attorney General of Ohio, is a sovereign State in the United States of America.

25B. The State of Kansas, by and through Derek Schmidt, Attorney General of Kansas, is a sovereign State in the United States of America.

25C. The State of Wyoming, by and through Matthew H. Mead, Governor of Wyoming, is a sovereign State in the United States of America.

25D. The State of Wisconsin, by and through J.B. Van Hollen, Attorney General of Wisconsin, is a sovereign State in the United States of America.

25E. The State of Maine, by and through William J. Schneider, Attorney General of Maine, is a sovereign State in the United States of America.

25F. Terry E. Branstad, Governor of Iowa, is bringing this action on behalf of the People of Iowa, a sovereign State in the United States of America.

26) The National Federation of Independent Business (NFIB), a California nonprofit mutual benefit corporation, is the nation's leading association of small businesses, including individual members, and has a presence in all 50 States and the District of Columbia. NFIB's mission is to promote and protect the rights of its members to own, operate, and earn success in their businesses, in accordance with lawfully-imposed governmental requirements. The NFIB Small Business Legal Center is a nonprofit, public interest law firm established to provide legal resources and be the voice for small businesses in the nation's courts through representation on issues of public interest affecting small businesses. NFIB's members include individuals who object to: forced compliance with the Act's mandate that they obtain qualifying healthcare insurance or pay a penalty; diversion of resources from their businesses that will result from complying with the mandate; and the Act's overreaching and unconstitutional encroachment on the States' sovereignty. NFIB joins in those objections on behalf of its members. NFIB's services to its members include providing information regarding legal and regulatory issues faced by small businesses, including individuals. NFIB will incur additional costs in assisting its members in understanding how the Act applies to them and affects their businesses.

27) Mary Brown is a citizen and resident of the State of Florida and a citizen of the United States. She is self-employed, operating Brown & Dockery, Inc., an automobile repair facility in Panama City, Florida, and is a member of NFIB. Ms. Brown has not had healthcare insurance for the last four years, and devotes her resources to maintaining her business and paying her employees. She does not qualify for Medicaid under the Act or Medicare and does not expect to qualify for them prior to the Act's individual mandate taking effect. Ms. Brown will be subject to the

mandate and objects to being forced to comply with it, and objects to the Act's unconstitutional overreaching and its encroachment on the States' sovereignty.

28) Kaj Ahlburg is a citizen and resident of the State of Washington and a citizen of the United States. Mr. Ahlburg has not had healthcare insurance for more than six years, does not have healthcare insurance now, and has no intention or desire to have healthcare insurance in the future. Mr. Ahlburg is and reasonably expects to remain financially able to pay for his own healthcare services if and as needed. He does not qualify for Medicaid under the Act or Medicare and does not expect to qualify for them prior to the Act's individual mandate taking effect. Mr. Ahlburg will be subject to the mandate and objects to being forced to comply with it, and objects to the Act's unconstitutional overreaching and its encroachment on the States' sovereignty. (Plaintiffs Brown and Ahlburg are referred to as the Individual Plaintiffs.)
29) The Department of Health and Human Services (HHS) is an agency of the United States, and is responsible for administration and enforcement of the Act, through its center for Medicare and Medicaid Services.
30) Kathleen Sebelius is Secretary of HHS, and is named as a party in her official capacity.
31) The Department of the Treasury (Treasury) is an agency of the United States, and is responsible for administration and enforcement of the Act.
32) Timothy F. Geithner is Secretary of the Treasury, and is named as a party in his official capacity.
33) The Department of Labor (DOL) is an agency of the United States, and is responsible for administration and enforcement of the Act.
34) Hilda L. Solis is Secretary of DOL, and is named as a party in her official capacity.

Factual Allegations

The Unprecedented and Unconstitutional Individual Mandate

35) The Act mandates that all persons who are citizens or legal residents of any State within the United States, including NFIB members and the Individual Plaintiffs, must have and maintain qualifying healthcare coverage, regardless of whether they wish to do so, to avoid having to pay a penalty. Many individuals, including NFIB members and the

Individual Plaintiffs, will be forced to purchase the required coverage with their own assets, without contribution or subsidy from the federal government. If a person fails to maintain such coverage, the federal government will force that person to pay a penalty, the amount of which will be increased gradually through 2016, reaching 2.5 percent of household income or $695 per year (up to a maximum of three times that amount ($2,085)) per family, whichever is greater. After 2016, the penalty will increase annually based on a cost-of-living adjustment.

36) Exemptions to the penalty apply for individuals with certain religious objections, individuals who belong to certain faith-based healthcare cooperative organizations, American Indians, persons without coverage for less than three months, undocumented immigrants, incarcerated individuals, persons for whom the lowest cost plan option exceeds 8 percent of income, individuals with incomes below the tax filing threshold, and persons with financial hardships. Millions of individuals will be forced to choose between having qualified coverage and paying the penalty.

37) Congress never before has imposed a mandate that all citizens buy something—in this case health insurance—or pay a penalty. According to the non-partisan Congressional Budget Office (CBO), "the imposition of an individual mandate [to buy health insurance] . . . would be unprecedented. The government has never required people to buy any good or service as a condition of lawful residence in the United States." THE BUDGETARY TREATMENT OF AN INDIVIDUAL MANDATE TO BUY HEALTH INSURANCE, CBO MEMORANDUM (August 1994), http://www.cbo.gov/ftpdocs/48xx/doc4816/doc38.pdf (last visited May 11, 2010). The CBO added that an individual mandate could "transform the purchase of health insurance from an essentially voluntary private transaction into a compulsory activity mandated by law." *Id.*

38) Congress lacks the constitutional authority to enact the individual mandate. The Constitution limits Congress's authority to the specific powers enumerated in Article I, and thus does not grant unlimited authority to Congress. None of Congress's enumerated powers includes the authority to force every American to buy a good or service on the private market or face a penalty. For the first time, Congress under the Act is attempting to regulate and penalize Americans for choosing not to engage in economic activity. If Congress can do this much, there will be virtually no sphere of private decision-making beyond the reach of federal power.

Medicaid Program Prior to the Act

39) Medicaid was established by Title XIX of the Social Security Act of 1965, 42 U.S.C. §§ 1396 *et seq.*, as the nation's major healthcare program for low-income persons. The States and the federal government have funded each participating State's Medicaid program jointly.

40) From the beginning of Medicaid until passage of the Act, the States were given considerable discretion to implement and operate their respective Medicaid programs in accordance with State-specific designs regarding eligibility, enrollment, and administration, so long as the programs met broad federal requirements.

41) At the outset of Medicaid, the States were free to opt in and establish their own State health or welfare plans or to provide no benefits at all. None of the Plaintiff States agreed to become a Medicaid partner of the federal government with an expectation that: a) the terms of its participation would be altered significantly; b) the federal government would increase significantly its own control and reduce significantly that State's discretion over the Medicaid program; c) the federal government would alter the program's requirements to expand eligibility for enrollment beyond the State's ability to fund its participation; d) the federal government would alter the program from requiring that States pay for healthcare services to requiring that States provide such services; or e) the federal government would exercise its control over Medicaid terms and eligibility as part of a coercive scheme to force all citizens and residents of the States to have healthcare coverage.

The Act's Injurious Impact on the Federal-State Healthcare Partnership

42) The Act greatly alters the federal-State relationship, to the detriment of the Plaintiff States, with respect to Medicaid programs, their insurance regulatory role, and healthcare coverage generally.

43) The Act transforms Medicaid from federal-State partnerships into a broad federally-controlled program that deprives the States of the ability to define healthcare program eligibility and attributes, and eliminates States' historic flexibility to make cost-saving and other adjustments to their respective Medicaid programs. The Act also sets new increased Medicaid rates for primary-care practitioners' reimbursements, which States must substantially fund, and changes the manner in which drug rebates are allocated between the federal government and States in a

manner that financially benefits the federal government at the States' expense.

44) The Act requires each State to expand massively its Medicaid program and to create a statewide exchange, which must be either a State governmental agency or a nonprofit entity established by the State for this purpose, through which the citizens and residents of that State can purchase healthcare insurance. If a State does not satisfy federal requirements to progress toward creation of an intrastate insurance exchange between now and the end of 2012, or chooses not to operate an exchange, the federal government (or its contractor) will establish and administer an intrastate exchange within that State. This action would displace State authority over a substantial segment of intrastate insurance regulation (e.g., licensing and regulation of intrastate insurers, plans, quality ratings, coordination with Medicaid and other State programs, and marketing) that the States have always possessed under the police powers provided in the Constitution, and subject the States to possible exchange-related penalties.

45) Participation in the Act will force the States to expand their Medicaid coverage to include all individuals under age 65 with incomes up to 133 percent of the federal poverty level. The federal government will fund much of the cost initially, but States' coverage burdens will increase significantly after 2016, both in actual dollars and in proportion to the contributions of the federal government.

46) The Act further requires that States provide healthcare services to enrollees, a significant new obligation that goes far beyond the States' pre-Act responsibility for funding healthcare services under their respective Medicaid programs. This obligation will expose the States to significant increased litigation risks and costs.

47) The federal government will not provide full funding or resources to the States to administer the Act. Each State must oversee the newly-created intrastate insurance market by instituting regulations, consumer protections, rate reviews, solvency and reserve fund requirements, and premium taxes. Each State also must enroll all of the newly-eligible Medicaid beneficiaries (many of whom will be subject to a penalty if they fail to enroll), coordinate enrollment with the new intrastate insurance exchange, and implement other specified changes. The Act further requires each State to establish a reinsurance program by 2014, to administer a premium review process, and to cover costs associated with

State-mandated insurance benefit requirements that States previously could impose without assuming a cost.

48) In addition, the Act imposes new requirements on the Plaintiff States that interfere with their ability to perform governmental functions. Effective in 2014, the Plaintiff States, as large employers, must automatically enroll employees working 30 or more hours a week into health insurance plans, without regard for current State practice, policy preferences, or financial constraints. The Act's individual mandate effectively will force many more State employees into State insurance plans than the Plaintiff States now allow, at a significant added cost to the States. Moreover, the States will be subject to substantial penalties and taxes prescribed by the Act, at a cost of thousands of dollars per employee, for State employees who obtain subsidized insurance from an exchange instead of from a State plan, or if the State plan offers coverage that is either too little or too generous as determined by the federal government. New tax reporting requirements prescribed by the Act also will burden the Plaintiff States' ability to source goods and services as necessary to carry out governmental functions.

The Act's Injurious Impact on Plaintiffs

49) The Act will have a profound and injurious impact on all Plaintiff States. Florida's circumstances, as described below, are not identical to the circumstances in all of the Plaintiff States, but fairly represent the nature of the burdens the Act imposes on the Plaintiff States.

50) Based on United States Census Bureau statistics from 2008, Florida has 3,641,933 uninsured persons living in the State. Of those persons, 1,259,378 are below 133 percent of the federal poverty line; therefore, the Act requires that Florida add them to its Medicaid rolls.

51) Even before passage of the Act, the Medicaid program imposed a heavy cost on Florida, consuming 26 percent of its annual budget. For fiscal year 2009-2010 alone, Florida will spend more than $18 billion on Medicaid, servicing more than 2.7 million persons. Florida's Medicaid contributions and burdens, from the implementation of its Medicaid program in 1970 to the present, have gradually increased to the point where it would be infeasible for Florida to cease its participation in Medicaid before the Act takes effect and make alternate arrangements for a traditional Medicaid-like program.

52) The federal government currently contributes 67.64 percent of every dollar Florida spends on Medicaid, a percentage that is temporarily inflated because of federal stimulus outlays. Under the current pre-Act program, after this year, the percentage of Florida's Medicaid expenses covered by the federal government would decline, and by 2011 would reach 55.45 percent, a level that is closer to the recent average. The federal government's contribution under the Act, though providing more aid for newly-eligible persons, will not fully compensate Florida for the dramatic increase to its Medicaid rolls, increased reimbursement rates for primary-care practitioners, and other substantial costs that it must bear under the Act.

53) Florida's Agency for Health Care Administration (AHCA) estimates that at least 80 percent of persons who have some form of health insurance but fall below 133 percent of the federal poverty level will drop their current plans and enroll in Medicaid, because they are newly eligible under the Act. The Act does not provide full funding for the States' cost of covering these already-covered persons. These persons represent a significant additional cost to Florida under the Act.

54) The Act also makes a large new class of persons eligible for Medicaid in Florida. Prior to passage of the Act, only certain specified low-income individuals and families qualified for Medicaid. Moreover, the qualifying income level set by Florida was generally much lower than the level of 133 percent of the federal poverty line set by the federal government under the Act. Now, Florida also must add to its Medicaid rolls every childless adult whose income falls below 133 percent of the federal poverty line, consistent with the Act's fundamental change in Medicaid from a federal-State partnership to provide a safety net for the needy into a federally-imposed regime for universal healthcare coverage.

55) Prior to passage of the Act, AHCA was Florida's designated State Medicaid agency tasked with developing and carrying out policies related to the Medicaid program. The Act will strip away much of the State's authority to establish and execute policies, transferring that authority to the federal government. Indeed, the Act renders AHCA and other Florida agencies mere arms of the federal government and commandeers and forces AHCA employees to administer what now is essentially a federal universal healthcare program.

56) AHCA projects a cost to Florida in the billions of dollars between now and 2019, stemming from Medicaid-related portions of the Act. The annual cost will continue to grow in succeeding years. AHCA's projections, moreover, understate the Act's adverse impact on Florida. They do not include estimated costs to be borne by Florida to administer the Act or to prepare for the Act's implementation. Such costs will include hiring and training new staff, creating new information technology infrastructures, developing an adequate provider base, creating a scheme for accountability and quality assurance, and incurring many other expenses.

57) The Act requires that Florida immediately begin to devote funds and other resources to implement sweeping changes across multiple agencies of government. Such implementation burdens include, but are not limited to: a) enforcing the Act's immediately-effective terms; b) determining gaps between current resources in State government and the Act's requirements; c) evaluating infrastructure to consider how new programs and substantial expansion of existing programs will be implemented (e.g., new agencies, offices, etc.); d) developing a strategic plan and coordinating common issues across State agencies; e) initiating legislative and regulatory processes, while at the same time monitoring and engaging the substantial federal regulatory processes to ensure that State interests are protected; f) electing whether to participate in optional programs set forth in the Act; g) satisfying the Act's interim targets; and h) developing a communications structure and plan to disseminate new information regarding changes brought about by the Act to the many affected persons and entities.

58) The Act further requires Florida to enroll in healthcare insurance plans categories of State employees not previously covered by State-funded healthcare insurance plans. The Act subjects the State to penalties, depending upon the coverage decisions made by its employees, and limits the State's ability to determine coverage. If the State's plan for its employees is deemed inadequate by the federal government, the State will be subject to penalties. If the State's plan is deemed too generous or expansive by the federal government, the State will be subject to a distinct federal tax liability.

59) The Act also requires that Florida be responsible for providing healthcare services for all Medicaid enrollees in the expanded program, a significant change from Florida's responsibility for

providing payment for such services. This added responsibility and resulting new legal liabilities further contribute to the Act's substantial and costly impact on Florida's fisc, and will force the State to ignore other critical needs, including education, corrections, law enforcement, and more.

60) In sum, as demonstrated through the effects on Florida, the Act infringes on the Plaintiff States' constitutional status as sovereigns, entitled to cooperate with but not to be controlled by the federal government under the Medicaid program.

61) In addition, the Act will have a profound and injurious impact on the Plaintiff States' citizens and residents, a significant number of whom are or will be subject to the Act's mandate to obtain qualifying healthcare coverage or pay a penalty.

62) The Act further will have a profound and injurious impact on NFIB's individual members and its uninsured small business owners, including Ms. Brown, who are and will continue to be subject to the Act's mandate to obtain qualifying healthcare coverage or pay a penalty. Because of the mandate, these members will be forced to divert resources from their business endeavors, or otherwise to reorder their economic circumstances, in order to obtain qualifying healthcare coverage, regardless of their own conclusions on whether or not obtaining and maintaining such coverage for themselves and their dependents is a worthwhile cost of doing business. The added costs of the mandate will threaten the members' ability to maintain their own, independent businesses.

63) An important service offered by NFIB to its membership is the provision of information and assistance regarding legal and regulatory compliance issues faced by small businesses, as well as questions involving healthcare insurance and benefits. In order fully to serve the needs and interests of its membership, NFIB now will be forced to devote its own scarce resources to assisting members in understanding how the Act, including the mandate to obtain qualifying coverage or pay a penalty, applies to them, how it will affect their businesses, and what they must do to comply.

64) The Act also will injure Mr. Ahlburg, who will be subject to the Act's mandate to obtain qualifying healthcare coverage or pay a penalty.

The Act's Requirements and Effects on the Plaintiff States Cannot Be Avoided

65) Plaintiff States cannot avoid the Act's requirements. Neither the Act nor current federal Medicaid provisions prescribe a mechanism for a State to opt out of the Act's new Medicaid requirements, to opt out of Medicaid generally, or to transition to another program that provides only traditional Medicaid services.

66) Moreover, if they were to end their longstanding participation in Medicaid, Plaintiff States would desert millions of their residents, leaving them without access to the healthcare services they have depended on for decades under Medicaid. Thus, Plaintiff States are forced to accept the harmful effects of the Act on their fiscs and their sovereignty.

67) Prior to passage of the Act, Medicaid and its corresponding law, regulations, guidance, policies, and framework had been well-established, subject to occasional limited modifications, for more than four decades. During that time, participating States developed their respective Medicaid programs in reliance on Medicaid continuing to be a partnership with the federal government.

68) Presently, the Centers for Medicare and Medicaid (CMS), the federal agency with chief responsibility for administering Medicaid for the federal government, will terminate a State's federal funding for Medicaid unless the State complies with the Act's requirements. In addition, Medicaid requirements are linked to other federal programs, and the benefits of those programs to a State and its citizens and residents would be in jeopardy if the federal government were to terminate the State's participation in Medicaid.

Causes of Action

Count One

Unconstitutional Mandate that All Individuals Have Healthcare Insurance Coverage or Pay a Penalty (Const. Art. I & Amend. Ix, X)

69) Plaintiffs reallege, adopt, and incorporate by reference paragraphs 1 through 68 above as though fully set forth herein.

70) The Act forces all Americans, including NFIB members and the Individual Plaintiffs, regardless of whether they want healthcare coverage, to obtain and maintain a federally-approved level of coverage or pay a penalty. The Act thus compels all Americans to perform an affirmative act or incur a penalty, simply on the basis that they exist and reside within any of the United States. In so doing, the Act purports to exercise the very type of general police power the Constitution reserves to the States and denies to the federal government.
71) The Act is directed to a lack of, or failure to engage in, activity that is driven by the choices of individual Americans. Such inactivity by its nature cannot be deemed to be in commerce or to have such an effect on commerce, whether interstate or otherwise, as to be subject to Congress's powers under the Commerce Clause, Const. art. I, § 8. Nor does the Act regulate (directly or indirectly) any properly regulable interstate or foreign market or other commerce, any instrumentality of interstate or foreign commerce, or the actual flow of goods, services, and human beings among the States. As a result, the Act cannot be upheld under the Commerce Clause.
72) The Act infringes upon Plaintiff States' sovereign interests by coercing many persons to enroll in an expanded Medicaid program at a substantial cost to Plaintiff States, or to obtain coverage from intrastate exchanges that States must establish to avoid loss of substantial regulatory authority. The Act also denies Plaintiff States their sovereign ability to confer rights upon their citizens and residents to make healthcare decisions without government interference, including the decision not to participate in any healthcare insurance program or scheme, in violation of the Ninth and Tenth Amendments to the Constitution and the constitutional principles of federalism and dual sovereignty on which this Nation was founded.
73) The Act's penalty on uninsured persons unlawfully coerces persons to obtain healthcare coverage without purposing to raise revenue and injures the Plaintiff States' fiscs, because many persons will be compelled to enroll in Medicaid at a substantial cost to Plaintiff States or to get coverage from intrastate exchanges that Plaintiff States must establish to avoid loss of substantial regulatory authority. As a result, the Act cannot be upheld under the Taxing and Spending Clause, Const. art. I, § 8.

74) By requiring and coercing citizens and residents of the Plaintiff States to have healthcare coverage, the Act exceeds Congress's limited powers enumerated in Article I of the Constitution, and cannot be upheld under any other provision of the Constitution.
75) By requiring and coercing citizens and residents of the Plaintiff States to have healthcare coverage, the Act deprives those citizens and residents, and NFIB members and the Individual Plaintiffs, of their rights under State law to make personal healthcare decisions without governmental interference, and violates the rights of the States as sovereigns to confer and define such rights in their constitutions or by statute, in violation of the Ninth and Tenth Amendments to the Constitution and the constitutional principles of federalism and dual sovereignty on which this Nation was founded.

WHEREFORE, Plaintiffs respectfully request that the Court:

A. Declare the Patient Protection and Affordable Care Act, as amended, to be unconstitutional;
B. Declare that the individual mandate exceeds Congress's authority under Article I of the Constitution and violates the Ninth and Tenth Amendments;
C. Enjoin Defendants and any other agency or employee acting on behalf of the United States from enforcing the Act against the Plaintiff States, including their agencies, officials, and employees; the citizens and residents of the Plaintiff States; NFIB members and small business owners; and the Individual Plaintiffs, and to take such actions as are necessary and proper to remedy their violations deriving from any such actual or attempted enforcement; and
D. Award Plaintiffs their costs and grant such other relief as the Court may deem just and proper.

Count Two

Unconstitutional Mandate that All Individuals Have Healthcare Insurance Coverage or Pay A Penalty (Const. Amend. V)

76) Plaintiffs reallege, adopt, and incorporate by reference paragraphs 1 through 68 above as though fully set forth herein.

77) The Act forces citizens and residents of the Plaintiff States, including NFIB members and the Individual Plaintiffs, to obtain and maintain a federally-approved level of health coverage for themselves and their dependents, regardless of whether they want or need that coverage, or pay a penalty.

78) By requiring and coercing NFIB's members and the Individual Plaintiffs to obtain and maintain such healthcare coverage, the Act deprives them of their right to be free of unwarranted and unlawful federal government compulsion in violation of the Due Process Clause of the Fifth Amendment to the Constitution of the United States.

WHEREFORE, Plaintiffs respectfully request that the Court:

A. Declare the Patient Protection and Affordable Care Act, as amended, to be unconstitutional;
B. Declare Defendants to have violated the rights of NFIB members and small business owners and the Individual Plaintiffs under the Due Process Clause of the Fifth Amendment;
C. Enjoin Defendants and any other agency or employee acting on behalf of the United States from enforcing the Act against NFIB members and small business owners and the Individual Plaintiffs, and to take such actions as are necessary and proper to remedy their violations deriving from any such actual or attempted enforcement; and
D. Award NFIB and the Individual Plaintiffs their costs and grant such other relief as the Court may deem just and proper.

Count Three

Violation of Constitutional Prohibition of Unapportioned Capitation or Direct Tax(Const. Art. I, §§ 2, 9 & Amends. Ix, X)

79) Plaintiffs reallege, adopt, and incorporate by reference paragraphs 1 through 68 above as though fully set forth herein.

80) Alternatively, the penalty on uninsured persons under the Act constitutes a capitation and a direct tax that is not apportioned among the States according to census data, thereby injuring the sovereign interests of Plaintiff States and the interests of all citizens and residents of the Plaintiff States and of the United States.

81) The tax applies without regard to property, profession, or any other circumstance, and is unrelated to any taxable event or activity. It is to be levied upon persons for their failure or refusal to do anything other than to exist and reside in any of the States comprising the United States.

82) The tax violates article I, sections 2 and 9 of, and the Ninth and Tenth Amendments to, the Constitution. The Act's imposition of the tax, and the resulting coercion of many persons either to enroll in an expanded Medicaid program at a substantial cost to the Plaintiff States or to get coverage from intrastate exchanges that States must establish to avoid loss of substantial regulatory authority, injures Plaintiff States' sovereign interests and violates the States' constitutional protection against unapportioned capitation taxes or direct taxation. The tax also infringes on the right of NFIB members and the Individual Plaintiffs to be free from unconstitutional taxation. The tax is unconstitutional on its face and cannot be applied constitutionally.

WHEREFORE, Plaintiffs respectfully request that the Court:

A. Declare the Patient Protection and Affordable Care Act, as amended, to be unconstitutional;
B. Declare Defendants to have violated the Plaintiff States' constitutional protection against unapportioned capitation taxes or direct taxation, and to have violated the rights of all citizens and residents of the Plaintiff States and of the United States, including NFIB members and small business owners and the Individual Plaintiffs, to be free from unconstitutional taxation;
C. Enjoin Defendants and any other agency or employee acting on behalf of the United States from enforcing the Act against the Plaintiff States, including their agencies, officials, and employees; the citizens and residents of the Plaintiff States; NFIB members and small business owners; and the Individual Plaintiffs, and to take such actions as are necessary and proper to remedy their violations deriving from any such actual or attempted enforcement; and
D. Award Plaintiffs their costs and grant such other relief as the Court may deem just and proper.

Count Four

Coercion And Commandeering as to Medicaid (Const. Art. I & Amends. Ix, X)

83) Plaintiffs reallege, adopt, and incorporate by reference paragraphs 1 through 68 above as though fully set forth herein.
84) Plaintiff States cannot afford the unfunded costs of participating under the Act, but effectively have no choice other than to participate.
85) The Act exceeds Congress's powers under Article I of the Constitution, and cannot be upheld under the Commerce Clause, Const. art. I, §8; the Taxing and Spending Clause, id.; or any other provision of the Constitution.
86) By using Medicaid to reach universal healthcare coverage goals and forcing fundamental changes in the nature and scope of the Medicaid program upon the Plaintiff States, by denying Plaintiff States any choice with respect to new Medicaid requirements and denying them flexibility to limit the fiscal impact of those changes, by effectively co-opting Plaintiff States' control over their budgetary processes and legislative agendas through compelling them to assume costs they cannot afford, by forcing Plaintiff States to become responsible for providing healthcare services for all Medicaid enrollees, by requiring Plaintiff States to carry out insurance mandates and establish intrastate insurance programs and regulations for federal purposes, by interfering in the Plaintiff States' relationships with their employees with respect to healthcare coverage, by commandeering the Plaintiff States and their employees as agents of the federal government's regulatory scheme at the States' own cost, and by interfering in the Plaintiff States' sovereignty, the Act violates Article IV, section 4 of the Constitution, depriving Plaintiff States of their sovereignty and their right to a republican form of government; violates the Ninth and Tenth Amendments; and violates the constitutional principles of federalism and dual sovereignty on which this Nation was founded.

WHEREFORE, Plaintiff States respectfully request that the Court:

A. Declare the Patient Protection and Affordable Care Act, as amended, to be unconstitutional;
B. Declare that the Act exceeds Congress' powers under Article I of the Constitution and interferes in the Plaintiff States' sovereignty in violation

of the Ninth and Tenth Amendments and constitutional principles of federalism and dual sovereignty;

C. Enjoin Defendants and any other agency or employee acting on behalf of the United States from enforcing the Act against the Plaintiff States, their citizens and residents, and any of their agencies or officials or employees, and to take such actions as are necessary and proper to remedy their violations deriving from any such actual or attempted enforcement; and

D. Award Plaintiff States their costs and grant such other relief as the Court may deem just and proper.

Count Five

Coercion and Commandeering as to Healthcare Insurance (Const. Art. I & Amends. Ix, X)

87) Plaintiffs reallege, adopt, and incorporate by reference paragraphs 1 through 68 above as though fully set forth herein.

88) By requiring the Plaintiff States to carry out insurance mandates and establish intrastate insurance programs for federal purposes under threat of removing or significantly curtailing their long-held regulatory authority as to intrastate insurance, and by commandeering the Plaintiff States and their employees as agents of the federal government's regulatory scheme at the States' own cost, the Act exceeds Congress's powers under Article I of the Constitution, and interferes in the Plaintiff States' sovereignty in violation of the Ninth and Tenth Amendments and the constitutional principles of federalism and dual sovereignty on which this Nation was founded.

WHEREFORE, Plaintiff States respectfully request that the Court:

A. Declare the Patient Protection and Affordable Care Act, as amended, to be unconstitutional;

B. Declare that the Act exceeds Congress' powers under Article I of the Constitution and interferes in the Plaintiff States' sovereignty in violation of the Ninth and Tenth Amendments and constitutional principles of federalism and dual sovereignty;

C. Enjoin Defendants and any other agency or employee acting on behalf of the United States from enforcing the Act against the Plaintiff States, their citizens and residents, and any of their agencies or officials or employees, and to take such actions as are necessary and proper to remedy their violations deriving from any such actual or attempted enforcement; and

D. Award Plaintiff States their costs and grant such other relief as the Court may deem just and proper.

Count Six

Interference with the States' Sovereignty as Employers and Performance of Governmental Functions (Const. Art. I & Amends. Ix, X)

89) Plaintiffs reallege, adopt, and incorporate by reference paragraphs 1 through 68 above as though fully set forth herein.

90) By imposing new employer healthcare insurance mandates on the Plaintiff States, by requiring that they automatically enroll and continue enrollment of employees in healthcare plans, by subjecting States to penalties and taxes depending upon plan attributes and individual employee coverage decisions, and by burdening the States' ability to procure goods and services and to carry out governmental functions, the Act exceeds Congress's powers under Article I of the Constitution, and interferes in the Plaintiff States' sovereignty in violation of the Ninth and Tenth Amendments and the constitutional principles of federalism and dual sovereignty on which this Nation was founded.

WHEREFORE, Plaintiff States respectfully request that the Court:

A. Declare the Patient Protection and Affordable Care Act, as amended, to be unconstitutional;

B. Declare that the Act exceeds Congress's powers under Article I of the Constitution, and interferes in the Plaintiff States' sovereignty in violation of the Ninth and Tenth Amendments and constitutional principles of federalism and dual sovereignty;

C. Enjoin Defendants and any other agency or employee acting on behalf of the United States from enforcing the Act against the Plaintiff States, their citizens and residents, and any of their agencies or officials or employees, and to take such actions as are necessary and proper to remedy their violations deriving from any such actual or attempted enforcement; and

D. Award Plaintiff States their costs and grant such other relief as the Court may deem just and proper.

Respectfully submitted,
PAMELA JO BONDI
ATTORNEY GENERAL OF FLORIDA

ALAN WILSON
ATTORNEY GENERAL OF SOUTH CAROLINA

JON BRUNING
ATTORNEY GENERAL OF NEBRASKA

GREG ABBOTT
ATTORNEY GENERAL OF TEXAS

MARK L. SHURTLEFF ATTORNEY GENERAL OF UTAH

JAMES D. "BUDDY" CALDWELL
ATTORNEY GENERAL OF LOUISIANA

LUTHER STRANGE
ATTORNEY GENERAL OF ALABAMA

BILL SCHUETTE
ATTORNEY GENERAL OF MICHIGAN

JOHN W. SUTHERS
ATTORNEY GENERAL OF COLORADO

THOMAS W. CORBETT, Jr.
GOVERNOR OF PENNSYLVANIA, and WILLIAM H. RYAN, Jr.,
ACTING ATTORNEY GENERAL OF PENNSYLVANIA

ROBERT M. McKENNA
ATTORNEY GENERAL OF WASHINGTON

LAWRENCE G. WASDEN
ATTORNEY GENERAL OF IDAHO

MARTY J. JACKLEY
ATTORNEY GENERAL OF SOUTH DAKOTA

GREGORY F. ZOELLER A
TTORNEY GENERAL OF INDIANA

WAYNE STENEHJEM
ATTORNEY GENERAL OF NORTH DAKOTA

HALEY BARBOUR
GOVERNOR OF MISSISSIPPI

JANICE K. BREWER
GOVERNOR OF ARIZONA, and
THOMAS C. HORNE, ATTORNEY
GENERAL OF THE STATE OF ARIZONA

JIM GIBBONS
GOVERNOR OF NEVADA

SAMUEL S. OLENS
ATTORNEY GENERAL OF GEORGIA

DANIEL S. SULLIVAN
ATTORNEY GENERAL OF ALASKA

MICHAEL DeWINE
ATTORNEY GENERAL OF OHIO

DEREK SCHMIDT
ATTORNEY GENERAL OF KANSAS

MATTHEW H. MEAD
GOVERNOR OF WYOMING

J.B. VAN HOLLEN
ATTORNEY GENERAL OF WISCONSIN

WILLIAM J. SCHNEIDER
ATTORNEY GENERAL OF MAINE

TERRY E. BRANSTAD
GOVERNOR OF IOWA

NATIONAL FEDERATION OF
INDEPENDENT BUSINESS

MARY BROWN

KAJ AHLBURG

/s/ Blaine H. Winship
Blaine H. Winship (Fla. Bar No. 0356913) Special Counsel
Joseph W. Jacquot (Fla. Bar No. 189715) Special Counsel
Scott D. Makar (Fla. Bar No. 709697) Solicitor General
Louis F. Hubener (Fla. Bar No. 0140084) Timothy D. Osterhaus
(Fla. Bar No. 0133728)
Deputy Solicitors General
Office of the Attorney General of Florida The Capitol, Suite PL-01
Tallahassee, Florida 32399-1050
Telephone: (850) 414-3300
Facsimile: (850) 488-4872
Email: blaine.winship@myfloridalegal.com Attorneys for Plaintiff States

Karen R. Harned
Executive Director
National Federation of Independent Business
Small Business Legal Center
1201 F Street, N.W., Suite 200
Washington, DC 20004
Telephone: (202) 314-2061
Facsimile: (202) 554-5572
Of counsel for Plaintiff National Federation of Independent Business

David B. Rivkin (D.C. Bar No. 394446)
Lee A. Casey (D.C. Bar No. 447443)
Baker & Hostetler LLP
1050 Connecticut Avenue, N.W., Ste. 1100
Washington, DC 20036
Telephone: (202) 861-1731

Facsimile: (202) 861-1783
Attorneys for Plaintiff States, National Federation of Independent Business, Mary Brown, and Kaj Ahlburg

Katherine J. Spohn
Special Counsel to the Attorney General
Office of the Attorney General of Nebraska
2115 State Capitol Building
Lincoln, Nebraska 68508
Telephone: (402) 471-2834
Facsimile: (402) 471-1929
Email: katie.spohn@nebraska.gov
Attorneys for Plaintiff the State of Nebraska

Bill Cobb
Deputy Attorney General
for Civil Litigation
Office of the Attorney General of Texas
P.O. Box 12548, Capitol Station
Austin, Texas 78711-2548
Telephone: (512) 475-0131
Facsimile: (512) 936-0545
Email: bill.cobb@oag.state.tx.us
Attorneys for Plaintiff the State of Texas

Clayton P. Kawski
Assistant Attorney General
Wisconsin Department of Justice
17 West Main Street
Madison, Wisconsin 53707
Telephone: (608) 266-7477
Facsimile: (608) 267-2223
Email: kawskicp@doj.state.wi.us
Attorneys for Plaintiff the State of Wisconsin

Certificate of Service

I hereby certify that, on this 18th day of January, 2011, a copy of the foregoing Second Amended Complaint was served on counsel of record for all Defendants through the Court's Notice of Electronic Filing system.

/s/ Blaine H. Winship
Blaine H. Winship
Special Counsel
Office of the Attorney General of Florida

In: Mandated Health Care: Constitutional Analysis ISBN: 978-1-61324-162-2
Editor: Jonathan P. Reilly © 2011 Nova Science Publishers, Inc.

Chapter 4

RELIGIOUS EXEMPTIONS FOR MANDATORY HEALTH CARE PROGRAMS: A LEGAL ANALYSIS*

Cynthia Brougher

SUMMARY

In March 2010, Congress enacted the Patient Protection and Affordable Care Act (PPACA), which included a provision that requires certain individuals to have a minimum level of health insurance. Additionally, the threat of bioterrorism has caused some to consider the possibility of introducing vaccination programs to prevent an outbreak of serious illnesses. Programs like health care coverage and vaccinations have the potential to violate certain religious beliefs and therefore may conflict with the First Amendment. In the continuing debate over issues for which mandatory health care programs might be solutions, questions have been raised about the constitutional issues relating to exemptions for health care programs.

For the purposes of this report, mandatory health care programs are those which require individuals to take some action relating to a health care policy objective. A variety of mandatory health care programs currently exists at the federal and state levels. Some programs are medical programs that require individuals to participate in a medical program, while some programs are financial programs that require individuals to pay for program

* This is an edited, reformatted and augmented version of a Congressional Research Services publication, dated May 26, 2010.

costs. For example, all 50 states and the District of Columbia require children to be vaccinated for certain illnesses and diseases before entering school. At the federal level, the tax system requires individuals to pay taxes that fund Medicare to provide health care to elderly citizens. In some instances, mandatory health care programs include exemptions that allow qualified persons to opt out of the required action. Specifically, religious exemptions have been provided in a variety of mandatory health care programs, including state immunization laws and Medicare taxes. These religious exemptions permit individuals who object to the program based on religious beliefs to avoid compromising those beliefs.

This report will discuss the legal issues that arise in the context of religious exemptions for mandatory health care programs. It will discuss constitutional and statutory provisions relating to religious protection and how such laws have been applied in the medical context. The report will also briefly address examples of health care programs that have included religious exemptions, including a discussion of the religious conscience exemption included in PPACA. It will analyze whether the U.S. Constitution requires religious exemptions for mandatory health care programs and whether, if not required, the Constitution allows religious exemptions for such programs.

INTRODUCTION

In March 2010, Congress enacted the Patient Protection and Affordable Care Act (PPACA), which included a provision that requires certain individuals to have a minimum level of health insurance.[1] Additionally, the threat of bioterrorism has caused some to consider the possibility of introducing vaccination programs to prevent an outbreak of serious illness. Programs like health care coverage and vaccinations have the potential to violate certain religious beliefs, which may conflict with the First Amendment. In the continuing debate over issues for which mandatory health care programs might be solutions, questions have been raised about the constitutional issues relating to exemptions for health care programs.

For the purposes of this report, mandatory health care programs are those which require individuals to take some action relating to a health care policy objective. A variety of mandatory health care programs currently exists at the federal and state levels. Some programs are medical programs that require individuals to participate in a program, while some programs are financial programs that require individuals to pay for program costs. For example, all 50 states and the District of Columbia require children to be vaccinated for certain illnesses and diseases before entering school. The federal tax system requires individuals to pay taxes that fund Medicare to provide health care to elderly citizens. In some instances, mandatory health care programs include exemptions which allow qualified persons to opt out of the required action. Religious exemptions have been provided in a variety of mandatory health care programs, including state immunization laws and Medicare taxes. These religious exemptions permit individuals who object to the program based on religious beliefs to avoid compromising their religious beliefs by not participating in the program.

This report will discuss the legal issues that arise in the context of religious exemptions for mandatory health care programs. It will discuss constitutional and statutory provisions relating to religious protection and how such laws have been applied in the medical context. The report will also briefly address examples of health care programs that have included religious exemptions, including a discussion of the religious conscience exemption included in PPACA. It will analyze whether the U.S. Constitution requires religious exemptions for mandatory health care programs and whether, if not required, the Constitution allows religious exemptions for such programs.

FREEDOM OF RELIGION IN A MEDICAL CONTEXT

General Constitutional and Statutory Protections of Religious Exercise

The First Amendment of the U.S. Constitution provides that "Congress shall make no law respecting an establishment of religion, or prohibiting the free exercise thereof...."[2] These clauses are known respectively as the Establishment Clause and the Free Exercise Clause. Although the U.S. Supreme Court had historically applied a heightened standard of review to government actions that allegedly interfered with a person's free exercise of religion,[3] the Court reinterpreted that standard in 1990. Since then, the Court has held that the Free Exercise Clause never "relieve[s] an individual of the obligation to comply with a valid and neutral law of general applicability."[4] Under this interpretation, the constitutional baseline of protection was lowered, meaning that laws that do not specifically target religion or do not allow for individualized assessments are not subject to heightened review under the Constitution.

Congress responded to the Court's holding by enacting the Religious Freedom Restoration Act (RFRA), which statutorily reinstated the standard of protection of heightened scrutiny for government actions interfering with a person's free exercise of religion.[5] When RFRA was originally enacted, it applied to federal, state, and local government actions, but the Supreme Court later ruled that its application to state and local governments was unconstitutional under principles of federalism.[6] RFRA provides that a statute or regulation of general applicability may lawfully burden a person's exercise of religion only if it (1) furthers a compelling governmental interest and (2) uses the least restrictive means to further that interest.[7] This standard is sometimes referred to as strict scrutiny analysis. The Supreme Court has held that in order for the government to prohibit exemptions to generally applicable laws, the government must "demonstrate a compelling interest in uniform application of a particular program by offering evidence that granting the requested religious accommodations would seriously compromise its ability to administer the program."[8]

Specific Free Exercise Rights Relating to Medical Treatment

Some religious doctrines forbid medical treatment or specific medical procedures.[9] Followers of these religions believe that receiving treatment would violate their First Amendment right to exercise their religion freely. This conflict raises the issue known as forced care—whether patients can be forced to receive medical care to which they otherwise would object on religious grounds. Legal issues of forced care typically arise in situations where patients lack the capacity to make an informed decision about whether or not to receive care. These situations often involve patients facing death if they do not receive treatment.[10] For example, because some religions have specific teachings regarding matters of life and death, a patient may object to life-saving treatment on religious grounds. However, if that patient lacks the capacity to provide informed consent at the time that care would be provided, a doctor or hospital may not be willing to withhold care based on religious affiliation alone, without an informed discussion with the patient.

Federal and state courts have addressed these issues of forced care for patients with religious objections to medical care. Caselaw indicates a growing willingness of courts over the past several decades to recognize patients' religious objections to medical care, including life-saving treatments. In the 1960s, a federal court authorized a hospital to treat a patient with what would be an objectionable procedure under her religion.[11] The patient faced death without a blood transfusion, a procedure that her religion prohibited, but due to emergency circumstances, the hospital staff was unable to determine if the patient was making an informed decision when she refused the treatment. By the 1980s, courts were giving greater weight to patients' choices regarding care.[12] In later cases, courts concluded that competent adults with religious objections to procedures cannot be forced to receive care, with one court noting that courts should give "great deference to the individual's right to make decisions vitally affecting his private life according to his own conscience."[13] It is important to note, however, that such deference to patients' objections to care may not be recognized in cases in which parents are claiming objections on behalf of a child.[14]

EXAMPLES OF RELIGIOUS EXEMPTIONS FOR HEALTH CARE PROGRAMS

Federal Health Insurance Coverage Requirements

The Patient Protection and Affordable Care Act (P.L. 111-148), enacted in March 2010, creates a requirement that individuals maintain insurance coverage.[15] This individual responsibility requirement (sometimes referred to as an individual mandate) requires that individuals and their dependents maintain "minimum essential coverage" after the effective date of the provision.[16] Individuals who do not maintain the required coverage face financial penalties for the months that they are not covered, if they do not qualify for one of the included exemptions.[17] PPACA includes a religious conscience exemption, which provides that the individual responsibility requirement does not apply to any individual who has been certified to be "a member of a recognized religious sect or division thereof described in section 1402(g)(1) [of the Internal Revenue Code of 1986] and an adherent of established tenets or teaching of such sect or division as described in such section."[18] Section 1402(g)(1) provides an exemption from self-employment income tax if the individual seeking exemption

> is a member of a recognized religious sect or division thereof and is an adherent of established tenets or teachings of such sect or division by reason of which he is conscientiously opposed to acceptance of the benefits of any private or public insurance which makes payments in the event of death, disability, old-age, or retirement or makes payments toward the cost of, or provides services for, medical care....[19]

Thus, there is no list of specific religious groups that qualify for the exemption. Rather, the exemption is general, such that any member of any religious organization with the beliefs described in the provision would qualify.[20]

This construction of the exemption conforms with the constitutional requirements of the First Amendment, as discussed later in this report.[21]

The exemption for religious groups with conscientious objections to medical treatment outside the religious community is typically associated with religious groups such as the Amish, which have historically opposed participation in public social service programs based on their religious beliefs. However, the exception is not specifically offered to that group, and speculation on which religious groups' tenets would qualify for exemption is beyond the scope of this report. Members of any religious group who can demonstrate conformance with the requirements of § 1402(g) would therefore be qualified for exemption under PPACA.

State Mandatory Vaccination Programs

As a matter of public health, all 50 states and the District of Columbia have enacted laws requiring vaccination, particularly in the context of school immunization laws.[22] These laws have been enacted under a rationale of preventing the spread of communicable and debilitating diseases. All but two states (Mississippi and West Virginia) have enacted religious exemptions for these vaccination programs. These exemptions allow students who have religious objections to the vaccinations, but would otherwise be required to be vaccinated, not to comply with the vaccination requirements.

These exemptions have raised constitutional questions related to free exercise rights, with many courts holding that exemptions are not required under the Free Exercise Clause. The U.S. Supreme Court has not ruled directly on the constitutionality of religious exemptions for these vaccination programs. However, the Court has addressed the conflict between public health policies and religious beliefs. Faced with such a conflict between the government's interest in protecting public health and individuals' interest in being free to exercise their religious beliefs, the Court has held in favor of public health concerns.[23] The implication that public health concerns outweigh the right to exercise one's religion without interference has led some state supreme courts to hold that mandatory vaccination programs are not a violation of religious freedom.[24]

The exemptions have also been challenged under the Establishment Clause and Equal Protection Clause. Allowing an exemption based on religion might appear to be endorsing a religion in violation of the Establishment Clause. Exemptions that allow certain individuals to claim religious objections to a process required for others also may give the appearance of distinct treatment for those individuals who have religious objections in violation of equal protection doctrine. Under the First Amendment, a law cannot favor some individuals based on their religious beliefs.[25] Allowing an exemption based on religion to a generally required practice may be construed as special treatment for religious adherents, particularly in cases in which the legal provisions limit the scope of the exemption to religious beliefs only (that is, excluding philosophical beliefs) or to members of specific religions only.[26] Because these exemptions seem to make a benefit available to religious adherents, but not to individuals who are not identified with that group, the exemptions also raise questions of equal protection under the Fifth or Fourteenth Amendment.[27] The Supreme Court of Mississippi, one of the states without a religious exemption, has held that requiring certain individuals to be vaccinated while still exposing them to exempted individuals is unconstitutional.[28]

Medicare Revenue Programs

The U.S. tax code includes several provisions that provide religious exceptions to certain revenue programs relating to health care. Specifically, the income "received for services performed by a member of a religious order in the exercise of duties required by the order"[29] is excepted from the Federal Insurance Contributions Act (FICA) tax, which funds Social Security and Medicare.[30] Also, ministers, members of religious orders, Christian Science practitioners, and members of religious faiths who oppose acceptance of insurance benefits, including medical care, are generally exempt from self-employment taxes.[31]

The U.S. Supreme Court has held that the Free Exercise Clause does not prohibit mandatory payment of social security taxes even when the payment of such taxes or the receipt of the related benefits would violate the taxpayer's religion. In *United States v. Lee*, a self-employed Amish man claimed that paying FICA taxes violated his belief in an obligation to provide similar assistance for church members.[32] Lee argued that his religion prohibited him from accepting such benefits from the state or paying taxes to fund the social security system. Although the Court recognized a burden on religious belief, it held that the burden was justified by the governmental interest in "maintaining a sound tax system," and that accommodation of all of the diverse religious beliefs relating to taxation would pose too great a difficulty to maintain a functional tax system.[33]

Massachusetts Comprehensive Health Care Program

In April 2006, Massachusetts enacted a comprehensive health care program that provides universal coverage for the state's residents.[34] The law requires employers to provide health insurance for employees and requires individuals to purchase insurance (through employers or individually). The state provides alternatives for employers and employees to facilitate the process of universal coverage. For example, employers that do not provide health insurance may instead pay into the state's uninsured care fund, and individuals who cannot afford coverage may be subsidized by the state. The law's individual mandate includes some exemptions (including a religious exemption), which allow individuals who meet certain qualifications effectively to opt out of the mandate to acquire insurance coverage.

To qualify for the religious exemption to the individual coverage requirement, an individual must file documentation with his or her tax return. The individual must state in the document "that his sincerely held religious beliefs are the basis of his refusal to obtain and maintain creditable coverage during the 12 months of the taxable year for which the return was filed."[35] If the individual received medical care during the year in which he claimed an exemption, he is responsible for paying for the care and is subject to penalty assessed by the commissioner of revenue.[36]

Constitutional Analysis of Religious Exemptions in Mandatory Health Care Programs

Religious exemption provisions in mandatory health care programs often raise constitutional issues of religious freedom and equal protection. Any religious exemption must meet the requirements of the First Amendment's religion clauses, which serve as guarantees that individuals will neither be required to act under a prescribed religious belief (the Establishment Clause) nor be prohibited from acting under their chosen religious beliefs (the Free Exercise Clause). Religious exemptions also may raise equal protection issues under the Fifth Amendment.

Thus, constitutional analysis of religious exemptions in mandatory health care programs must address two questions: (1) whether the Constitution requires a religious exemption to ensure the free exercise rights of citizens who may have religious objections to a mandatory program, and (2) if a religious exemption is not constitutionally required, but included nonetheless, whether it would be constitutional under the First and Fifth Amendments.

Does the Constitution Require a Religious Exemption for Mandatory Health Care Programs?

Any congressional enactment regarding mandatory health care programs would be subject to constitutional rules and would qualify for review under RFRA as a federal action that potentially burdens religious exercise. Thus, any legislation that would mandate a health care program would be subject to strict scrutiny analysis.

Generally, it does not appear that the U.S. Constitution requires a religious exemption with respect to legislation that creates mandatory health care programs, but the details of that legislation may impact the analysis. Under strict scrutiny, an exemption would be required only if the government does not have a compelling state interest that is achieved by the least restrictive means possible. The U.S. Supreme Court and other lower courts generally have allowed federal mandates that relate to public health, but nonetheless interfere with religious beliefs, to continue without exemptions.[37] In addressing the issue of religious objections to generally applicable public health requirements, the Supreme Court has upheld legislative acts that promote public policies relating to public health as a valid exercise of protecting the welfare of the people.[38] The government's interest in protecting public health has been held to outweigh individuals' religious interests. According to the Court, "the right to practice religion freely does not include liberty to expose the community or the child to communicable disease or the latter to ill health or death."[39] The Court's decision to hold the interest of public health above the interest of individuals to freely exercise their religious belief was made before the Court applied strict scrutiny to religious exercise cases, but nonetheless provides an indication of the nature of the government's interest in public health regulation. The Court has also held that the government's interest in tax programs used to fund health care programs outweighs individuals' interests in exercising their religion freely.[40] The Court's treatment of public health as an interest paramount to individual religious practice appears to open the door to recognition of public health as a compelling state interest under strict scrutiny analysis.

A mere connection to public health is not necessarily enough to find a compelling interest. Some courts have addressed the issues of religious exemptions in the context of certain mandatory health care programs, but the nature of other programs may lead to different outcomes. Laws that require an affirmative participation in a medical procedure (e.g., vaccination) differ from laws that require a more indirect participation in medical programs (e.g., funding for insurance programs). One factor that might affect the outcome of the constitutional analysis is the role the federal government plays in the objective of the program. Public health has historically been a matter of state regulation.[41] The vaccination laws were enacted under states' authority to regulate the public health of their citizens. The federal government, however, does have some authority to act in the realm of public health.[42] Also, the actual connection to public health might affect whether the government's interest is compelling. For example, although courts have recognized a compelling state interest in statutes preventing the spread of disease, it may be more difficult to find a compelling state interest in requiring individuals to have health insurance. Thus, the government's interest may vary depending on the specific requirements imposed by the legislation.

If the legislation does further a compelling governmental interest, it must also use the least restrictive means. That is, the government must make the burden as narrow as possible. This test may be met by providing alternative means of compliance with the legislation. In the context of the vaccination laws, for example, the government might allow individuals with religious objections to vaccination requirements to be quarantined or isolated to avoid infecting others, rather than receive the vaccination. In the context of universal health care insurance, the government might allow an exemption for individuals with religious objections and also allow individuals who objected without qualifying religious reasons to pay into a state fund rather than receive insurance coverage. These types of accommodations may be deemed the least restrictive means of advancing the government's interest because they satisfy both the individual's free exercise of religion and the government's interest in protecting public health. There may be other accommodations that would satisfy the requirement of tailoring the legislation narrowly to meet strict scrutiny requirements.

Thus, when determining whether a mandatory health care program would require a religious exemption, two factors are critical to the outcome of the analysis. First, the constitutionality would depend on the nature of the mandatory health care program (e.g., whether it is a required medical procedure or a required payment for an insurance program). Second, the constitutionality would depend on the structure of the program (e.g., whether the program provides the required participants options with which to comply in order to meet the program objectives). These factors would affect the extent of the burden placed on an individual's religious exercise and significantly impact the strict scrutiny analysis.

Does the Constitution Allow a Religious Exemption for Mandatory Health Care Programs?

Because legislation that mandates participating in health care programs may conflict with religious beliefs, Congress may choose to include an exemption for relevant religious objections even if it is not required. The exemption would provide an alternative for certain people based on their religious belief that would not be available to other people who do not share that religious belief. Thus, some individuals may claim that the exemption violates the Establishment Clause (by providing a benefit to groups based on religion) and the Equal Protection Clause (by providing for disparate treatment of separate groups).

The Establishment Clause prohibits preferential treatment of one religion over another or preferential treatment of religion generally over nonreligion.[43] Providing an exemption based on religion may be construed as favoring a particular religion or religion generally because only individuals with religious affiliation would be eligible for the exemption. However, the mere fact that a law addresses religion does not automatically make that law unconstitutional. Under Establishment Clause analysis, a government action must meet a three-part test known as the *Lemon* test. To meet the *Lemon* test, a law must (1) have a secular purpose, (2) have a primary effect that neither advances nor inhibits religion, and (3) not lead to excessive entanglement with religion.[44] The Supreme Court has upheld religious exemptions for government programs, where the exemptions were enacted to prevent government interference with religious exercise.[45]

Like the analysis under the Free Exercise Clause, the constitutionality of a religious exemption under the *Lemon* test would depend on the language of the exemption. Exemptions that are specifically available only to certain religions have been construed in some cases as a violation of the Establishment Clause.[46] However, providing an exemption that does not specify certain religions as eligible may not pass the *Lemon* test either. A generally available religious exemption may be construed as a violation of the Establishment Clause because it provides preferential treatment to individuals with religious beliefs, but does not provide individuals who might object on philosophical grounds to claim the exemption.[47] Thus, there does not appear to be a clear consensus regarding the constitutionality of religious exemptions under the Establishment Clause.

The concerns of preferential treatment for certain groups of individuals that lead to Establishment Clause questions also raise questions under the Equal Protection Clause. The Equal Protection Clause prevents the government from treating some groups of individuals differently than other groups of individuals. If the disparate treatment results from a "suspect classification," the Equal

Protection Clause may be violated. Typically, courts have recognized groups identified by race, national origin, or alienage as suspect classifications. In the context of religious exemptions, the group being treated differently is a group that might be based on religion or might be based on nonreligion. Often, courts decide cases alleging disparate treatment involving religion under the First Amendment, rather than equal protection. Thus, equal protection jurisprudence does not appear to have addressed religious discrimination to a significant extent. Courts have generally held that laws that treat groups of individuals differently because of some animus would be suspect classifications that would be subject to strict scrutiny. Thus, it appears that the analysis under the doctrine of equal protection likely would not produce a different outcome than the analysis that would be used under the First Amendment.

End Notes

[1] Patient Protection and Affordable Care Act, P.L. 111-148, § 1501(b) (2010), as amended by the Health Care and Education Reconciliation Act of 2010, P.L. 111-152, § 1002 (2010).

[2] U.S. Const. Amend. I. For discussion of the constitutional and statutory standards of review used in relation to the free exercise clause, see CRS Report RS22833, *The Law of Church and State: General Principles and Current Interpretations*, by Cynthia Brougher.

[3] *See* Wisconsin v. Yoder, 406 U.S. 205 (1972); Sherbert v. Verner, 374 U.S. 398 (1963).

[4] Employment Div., Oregon Dep't of Human Resources v. Smith, 494 U.S. 872, 879 (1990).

[5] P.L. 103-141, 103d Cong., 1st Sess. (November 16, 1993); 42 U.S.C. § 2000bb *et seq.*

[6] City of Boerne v. Flores, 521 U.S. 407 (1997).

[7] 42 U.S.C. § 2000bb-1(b). In some instances, RFRA may be preempted by another federal law. *See* S.Rept. 103-111, at 12-13 (1993) (stating that "nothing in this act shall be construed as affecting religious accommodation under title VII of the Civil Rights Act of 1964").

[8] Gonzales v. O Centro Espirita Beneficente Unaio Do Vegetal, 546 U.S. 418, 435-437 (2006).

[9] For example, two religious affiliations that often are involved in these types of cases are Jehovah's Witnesses and Christian Scientists. Jehovah's Witnesses believe that blood transfusions are prohibited by religious teachings. *Jehovah's Witnesses*, 7 Encyclopedia of Religion 4820 (Lindsay Jones, ed., 2nd ed.) (2005). Christian Scientists believe in the use of prayer, rather than medicine, to treat ailments. *Christian Science*, 1 Encyclopedia of Politics and Religion 141 (Robert Wuthnow, ed., 2nd ed.) (2006).

[10] The so-called "right to die" is beyond the scope of this report. For legal analysis on individuals' rights to decide the manner of death, see CRS Report 97-244, *The "Right to Die": Constitutional and Statutory Analysis*, by Kenneth R. Thomas.

[11] Application of the President and Directors of Georgetown College, 331 F.2d 1000 (D.C. Cir. 1964).

[12] *See, e.g.*, Bartling v. Superior Court, 163 Cal.App.3d 186 (Cal. Ct. App. 1984) ("patient's self-determination as to his own medical treatment ... must be paramount to the interests of the patient's hospital and doctors").

[13] Public Health Trust of Dade County v. Wons, 541 So.2d 96 (Fla. 1989); *see also* Norwood Hospital v. Munoz, 409 Mass. 116 (1991).

[14] In some cases when a child does not receive medical care based on the parents' religious objections, the parents may be held criminally or civilly liable for neglect or other related grounds. *See, e.g.,* Walker v. Superior Court, 763 P.2d 852 (1988). *Cf.* State v. Lockhart, 664 P.2d 1059 (Okla. Crim. App. 1983). *See also* Lundman v. McKown, 530 N.W.2d 807 (Minn. Ct. App. 1995).

[15] P.L. 111-148, § 1501. For a constitutional analysis of the individual responsibility requirement, *see* CRS Report R40725, *Requiring Individuals to Obtain Health Insurance: A Constitutional Analysis*, by Jennifer Staman et al. 16 § 5000A(a) of Subtitle D of the Internal Revenue Code of 1986, as amended by P.L. 111-148, § 1501.

[17] *Id.* at § 5000A(b).

[18] The religious conscience exemption is provided by section 5000A(d)(2)(A) of the Internal Revenue Code of 1986, as amended by § 1501 of PPACA.

[19] 26 U.S.C. § 1402(g)(1).

[20] The Supreme Court has held that legislation providing protection or exemption for a specific religious group may violate the Establishment Clause, which forbids preferential treatment based on religion. *See* Board of Education of Kiryas Joel v. Grumet, 512 U.S. 687 (1994) (invalidating the creation of a school district for one particular religious group). The Court has looked at whether the religious group alleged to be favored by the act in violation of the Establishment Clause is one of many religious groups eligible for similar treatment or if the special treatment is made through a series of benefits offered separately to multiple groups. *Id.* at 703-704.

[21] For a comprehensive constitutional analysis of the religious conscience exemption in the context of PPACA generally, *see* CRS Report R40725, *Requiring Individuals to Obtain Health Insurance: A Constitutional Analysis*, by Jennifer Staman et al.

[22] "State Vaccination Requirements," Centers for Disease Control and Prevention, *available at* http://www.cdc.gov/ vaccines/vac-gen/laws/state-reqs.htm. For more information on vaccination laws, see CRS Report RS21414, *Mandatory Vaccinations: Precedent and Current Laws*, by Kathleen S. Swendiman.

[23] Prince v. Commonwealth of Massachusetts, 321 U.S. 158 (1944).

[24] *See, e.g.*, Cude v. State, 237 Ark. 927 (1964).

[25] *See, e.g.*, Lynch v. Donnelly, 465 U.S. 668, 687 (1984) (O'Connor, J., concurring).

[26] *See, e.g.*, Boone v. Boozman, 217 F.Supp.2d 938 (E.D. Ark. 2002).

[27] The Fifth Amendment applies to federal government actions, while the Fourteenth Amendment applies to the states.

[28] Brown v. Stone, 376 So.2d 218 (Sup. Ct. Miss. 1979).

[29] Rev. Proc. 91-20, 1991-1 C.B. 524.

[30] 26 U.S.C. § 3121(b)(8).

[31] *See* 26 U.S.C. § 1402(e) and (g).

[32] 455 U.S. 252 (1982).

[33] *Id.* at 259-60.

[34] An Act Providing Access to Affordable, Quality, Accountable Health Care, MASS. GEN. LAWS ch. 58, § 12.

[35] MASS. GEN. LAWS ch. 111M, § 3.

[36] *Id.*

[32] 455 U.S. 252 (1982).

[33] *Id.* at 259-60.

[34] An Act Providing Access to Affordable, Quality, Accountable Health Care, MASS. GEN. LAWS ch. 58, § 12.

[35] MASS. GEN. LAWS ch. 111M, § 3.

[36] *Id.*

[37] *See, e.g.*, Prince v. Massachusetts, 321 U.S. 158 (1944); Cude v. State, 237 Ark. 927 (1964).

[38] Jacobson v. Massachusetts, 197 U.S. 11 (1905) (seminal case regarding state's authority to institute a mandatory vaccination program as a part of its police powers).

[39] *Prince*, 321 U.S. at 166-67.

[40] *Lee*, 455 U.S. at 260-61.

[41] *See* Gibbons v. Ogden, 22 U.S. 1 (1824) (addressing divisions of federal and state power).

[42] Federal jurisdiction to regulate public health derives from the Commerce Clause. U.S. CONST. art. I, § 8. The federal government has had a significant role in some public health matters, including food safety agencies, biomedical research programs, and health and safety regulatory programs.

[43] Epperson v. Arksansas, 393 U.S. 97, 103-04 (1968). *See also* Wallace v. Jaffree, 472 U.S. 38, 52-54 (1985); School Dist. of Abington Township v. Schempp, 374 U.S. 203, 216-217 (1963).

[44] Lemon v. Kurtzman, 403 U.S. 602, 612-13 (1971). While the first two prongs of the test are self-explanatory, the third prong prohibits "an intimate and continuing relationship" between government and religion as the result of the law. *Id.* at 621-22. The continuing viability of *Lemon* has been unclear as the Court has raised questions regarding its adequacy in analyzing these issues. *See, e.g.*, County of Allegheny v. American Civil Liberties Union, 492 U.S. 573 (1989).

[45] The Court in Locke v. Davey, 540 U.S. 712 (2004), recognized that some government actions that allow free exercise consequently raise questions of establishment, noting that there was room for "play in the joints" in this intersection of the religion clauses.

[46] *See* Sherr v. Northport-East Northport Union Free School District, 672 F. Supp. 81, 89-90 (E.D.N.Y. 1987).

[47] *See* McCarthy v. Boozman, 212 F.Supp. 2d 945 (W.D. Ark. 2002).

INDEX

A

B

C

D

E

F

G

H

N

O

P

Q

R

S

T

U

V

W

Y